For God So
LOVED

For God So
LOVED

A Lenten Devotional

About the Authors

For your journey through Lent this year, we've brought you a daily devotional that blends the intergenerational voices of astute leaders of the church to guide you on a meaningful pilgrimage to the cross and beyond, to resurrection.

DAN BOONE is the president of Trevecca Nazarene University. He earned MDiv and DMin degrees from Nazarene Theological Seminary and McCormick Theological Seminary. He has authored several books, including *Seven Deadly Sins*, the *Charitable Discourse* series, and, most recently, a daily devotional titled *You Say You Want a Revolution?*. Boone lives in Nashville with his wife, Denise.

SAMANTHA CHAMBO is a fervent preacher and teacher of the Word, traveling to and speaking at various district assemblies and NMI conventions worldwide for the Church of the Nazarene. She is the former coordinator of Nazarene Women Clergy for the Africa Region and was a lecturer at Nazarene Theological College in South Africa. Chambo holds a master's degree in theology from the University of Manchester and is working on her PhD in biblical studies from the same institute.

TARA BETH LEACH is the senior pastor of First Church of the Nazarene in Pasadena, California. She holds a BA from Olivet Nazarene University and an MDiv from Northern Theological Seminary. Leach is the author of *Emboldened* and *Kingdom Culture*.

JEREN ROWELL is the president of Nazarene Theological Seminary in Kansas City, Missouri. Before that, he served as district superintendent for the Kansas City District of the Church of the Nazarene, and he also pastored for more than twenty-five years. Dr. Rowell has written and contributed to numerous books and publications, including a previous Lenten devotional, *These Forty Days*.

Contents

ASH WEDNESDAY

March 6, 2019

written by Dan Boone

Read

Isaiah 58:1–12

Additional: Joel 2:1–2, 12–17 • Psalm 51:1–17 •
Matthew 6:1–6, 16–21 • 2 Corinthians 5:20b–6:10

Reflect

Seasons like Lent often have me looking for a higher spiritual gear. You know: slow down, read more Scripture, pray, and journal more often. It's as if I want to make myself better for God—as if that would somehow be impressive. The curse of a Christianity that is deeply personal is that it is often only that: deeply personal. And we have plenty "just Jesus and me" songs to reinforce the idea of this intimately personal relationship, which it is. But if personal is all it is, then God becomes more and more utilitarian, there to hear *my* prayers and meet *my* needs and tend to *my* vested interests.

Isaiah 58 could well be the antidote to this religious illness. We survived Isaiah 40–55, where the prayer of the people was, "Get us out of Babylon and back home to Jerusalem, where we can be in charge of our own lives." God moved through Cyrus the Persian, and now they *are* back home in Jerusalem—where they find their city in shambles, the economy tanked, the government weak, the GNP abysmal, and the poor rattling tin cups on every corner. So they double down on their religious practices, expecting God to improve things for them.

Yet God has a message for them. Beginning in Isaiah 56 and continuing into chapter 58, we hear the corrective judgment of God. It goes like this: *You worship me, claiming to desire my ways. You feign righteousness. You claim a privileged nearness to me. You fast and pray but do not get what you are after. Then you wonder what I am up to, why I don't respond as you ask. So let me tell you why. You are not seeking my delight. You are fasting for your own vested interests. The kind of fast I want from you is one that will result in freedom for the poor and the vulnerable among you. They will share your bread, your homes, and your clothes. They will have more. You will have less. If you do these things, then your light will shine in the darkness of your broken city, your bones will be made strong, and you will be like a watered garden.*

Maybe a new definition of Lenten time and space should be "the place where God tells us what we need to hear but don't wish to hear." In so many of our religious practices, we are primarily concerned with how we look in the eyes of God, with our appearance before God, with the impression we are making on God. Could it be that God is less interested in how we look and more interested in how we see the world around us? As long as "I" reside as the focal point of my religious practices, I will attend to *being seen.* But when the focal point of prayer and fasting becomes the world that God longs to redeem, then I will attend to *seeing* the hungry, the homeless, the naked, the oppressed, and the vulnerable among us. The delight of the Lord is that God's people see these. And when *they* become the focal point of our fasting and prayers, "Then you shall call, and the Lord will answer; you shall cry for help, and he will say, Here I am" (Isa. 58:9, NRSV).

As we begin our journey to the cross with Jesus—the Suffering Servant of God—it would do us well to remember that the first Lenten journey was not one of pious escape, mountain solitude, or reflective quietness. Jesus went to cities where people, along with their problems, presented themselves: an unfair taxation system, exclusive religion, poverty, sickness, self-interest, political gamesmanship. Jesus found delight in tending to the Father's business in the broken cities filled with human need. And in the private moment that is recorded in the Gethsemane prayer, he feels the weight of this kind of worshipful living and asks for the cup to pass. Yet, in asking, he recognizes that the delight of the Father is felt by the one who tends to the work of the kingdom. He bows his head and returns to the crowd, that mass of angry humanity who only knows how to seek its own vested interest.

Pray

Gracious God, speak your truth to us as you did to our brothers and sisters in Isaiah 58. May we have ears to hear what you desire of us during this Lenten season. Amen.

MARCH 7, 2019

written by Dan Boone

Read

Psalm 91:1–2, 9–16

Additional: Exodus 5:10–23 • Acts 7:30–34

Reflect

I can pretty much quote this psalm in its entirety. I heard it hundreds of times in our family devotions as a boy growing up in Mississippi. It was my dad's memorized Psalm. On nights that called for abbreviated family devotions, he quoted this text. He is now in his nineties with the full intent of hitting one hundred. And, given how stubborn we Boones are, I won't be surprised if he makes it.

Dad is a World War II veteran. He served as a medic in the Army and fought as a soldier in the Pacific Islands. Buried in his memorabilia drawer is a Silver Star for Valor on the Field of Combat. He often went into enemy fire to rescue and bring wounded soldiers to safety. It is a time in his life that he does not like to recall. The thing I heard him say most often was, "I did this so my children would not have to."

Psalm 91 went with him to the Pacific and back. He prayed it every night in a tent or foxhole. Placing it in that context transforms it into a liturgy of divine protection. The language befits impending destruction: "For he will deliver you from . . . deadly pestilence; he will cover you with his pinions and under his wings you will find refuge; . . . You will not fear the terror of the night, or the arrow that flies by day . . . A thousand may fall at your side, ten thousand at your right hand, but it will not come near you. Because you have made the LORD your refuge . . . no evil shall befall you. . . . I will protect those who know my name. . . . With long life I will satisfy them" (vv. 3–5, 7, 9–10, 14, 16, NRSV). This psalm assures the one who prays it that God is looking out for them.

I understand the danger of implying that divine protection is promised to the righteous in battle while the rest are left to the luck of the trajectories of bullets. I am not suggesting a theodicy based on a magic prayer. What I am suggesting is that life leads us to places where this psalm is a gift to be uttered by those who realize that our lives are ultimately in the hands of God. My dad was there as a young man during World War II. Jesus was there in the wilderness temptations as the force of darkness used every imaginable offer to divert him from his kingdom mission.

Hungry from the fast, weakened by the wilderness, and confronted by the adversary of all humanity, Jesus did hand-to-hand combat with the devil. I wasn't there, but I like to imagine Jesus quoting Psalm 91, like my Dad in a foxhole, to remind himself that he was not alone in battle. The devil tempted him to leap off the temple into the arms of the waiting angels, quoting Psalm 91 himself (v. 11; see also Matt. 4:6). I think Jesus smiled because the devil stopped at verse 12 and did not go on to the next verse, where the faithful one of God stomps on the head of the snake.

Our Lenten journey will take us into fierce battles where the outcome is neither guaranteed nor predetermined. And we can be sure that there is darkness filled with deadly intent ahead. Psalm 91 is a good companion prayer for a foxhole or a fight with dark powers. It is also helpful anytime we imagine over-whelming darkness and impending death. I'm sure Jesus prayed it often on his Lenten journey. Let's join him.

Pray

Gracious God, may our journey into the darkness of a world that practices crucifixion be accompanied by your assurance that evil will not have the last word. Amen.

Read

Exodus 6:1–13

Additional: Psalm 91:1–2, 9–16 • Acts 7:35–42

Reflect

I was burdened for a young man in our church whose life was one bad decision after another. Several times I tried to pray with him, and he allowed it because he respected me. Nevertheless, I never saw any change in him. He just continued in his ways. I shared my concern with a wise elder, who said something I haven't forgotten: "He isn't tired of being lost yet. Stay close. One day he will want another option. Some are not ready to hear the good news."

How do we travel the world offering the hope of salvation, only to find rejection from those who need it most? I would like to think that on any given day, anyone would be ready to respond to the message of Jesus, but apparently not. Maybe Exodus 6 can help us.

The people of God have been under the heavy hand of Pharaoh and his empire-building demands for so long that they cannot imagine a different future. They have acclimated themselves to the plight of the powerless. Even though they groan for relief and complain about the bitterness of slavery, they have stopped believing that freedom is possible for the likes of them. They pray prayers of deliverance without the accompanying expectation that anything will happen.

And then God burns a bush in Midian and sends a bored sheep tender back to the dark land of Egypt, where he once made a bad decision and possibly had a rap sheet waiting for him. This is a journey Moses would prefer to skip. He wants out in the worst way, but God won't take no for an answer. After several excuses, a magic snake stick, and some promised help, Moses finally goes down into Egypt on a mission from God.

After the story has gone a few chapters, we find Moses declaring the message of God to the slaves: "I am the Lord, and I will free you from the burdens of the Egyptians and deliver you from slavery to them. I will redeem you with an outstretched arm and with mighty acts of judgment. I will take you as my people, and I will be your God. . . . I will bring you into the land that I swore to give to Abraham, Isaac, and Jacob; I will give it to you for a possession. I am the Lord" (Exod. 6:6–8, NRSV).

I can't imagine better news for slaves. Like my bad-decision friend, you would think they'd be ready and open for this good news, but that is not so. "Moses told this to the Israelites; but they would not listen to Moses, because of their broken spirit and their cruel slavery" (v. 9, NRSV). Moses explains to the Lord that the people are not listening to him, and he even suggests the reason is that he is such a poor speaker. This is not the first time Moses has confessed his preaching deficiency. Aaron is the immediate result, a preaching sidekick who can really bring the word. But as I read through the rest of Exodus, a lack of persuasive preaching doesn't seem to be the problem. Sometimes people can't see a preferred future because of a broken spirit and cruel oppression. When the dark powers that run a dying world have done their number on you for a long, long time, believing the good news is hard.

It is interesting to compare the call of Moses to the call of Jesus. They both go on a journey for the salvation of the people of God. On the Lenten journey of Jesus, many were ripe and ready to believe that God was on the move to set them free. But there was as much blindness as belief.

Jesus invites us to be faithful on the journey, even if those we encounter are not ready for the good news. It may have nothing to do with the way we say it. It may be that a broken spirit needs tending.

Pray

Gracious God, grant us perseverance in the face of hearts so heavy and spirits so broken that imagination has been crucified. May the faithfulness of Jesus be our hope along the way. Amen.

SATURDAY
MARCH 9, 2019

written by Dan Boone

Read

Ecclesiastes 3:1–8

Additional: Psalm 91:1–2, 9–16 • John 12:27–36

Reflect

I had hoped my flight would be empty. I was tired and wanted to stretch out and sleep. But when you fly Southwest Airlines, your chances are slim. I was number 57 of 120. Not bad. Maybe the center seats would be vacant. I got on and went for the first window seat. It was in the front row, which faced backward. Our little two-row cubicle held six passengers, two beside me and three in front of me. Beside me was a young couple disgustingly tanned from their Florida vacation.

An elderly couple took the two seats immediately in front of me. He wore a fishing hat, blue jeans, and a green sport shirt. He was tall and had the look of a man who had worked hard his whole life. He sat with one hand over the other, trying to control the telltale shaking of Parkinson's disease. He had trouble with his Coke and peanuts. His wife had a puffy face, thinning hair, and reddened scalp. Her cough was deep. Large purple spots on her hands and arms suggested she had seen plenty of IVs. Lung cancer, she told me—three years ago, but now it was back.

They were going home to their daughter in Louisville following a visit with their other daughter in Orlando. While they had been in Orlando, the Louisville daughter had sold their house, downsized their belongings, auctioned off their antiques, and moved what was left into assisted-care living quarters. They would land, get off the plane, and go to a place they had never seen except in brochure pictures.

I decided to go beyond the obvious and asked, "How do you feel about this move?" They explained that they really didn't have a choice—his Parkinson's, her cancer, their age. They were coming to terms with what was to come. Our row got quiet. As we began our descent into Louisville, I watched their eyes as they looked out the small window and down onto the last chapter of their life. She reached over to steady his shaking hands. He returned the gesture with a smile of warm assurance that things would be okay. As they gathered their things to leave the plane, I reached over and touched his hand. "The Lord be with you," I said.

His reply still resonates with me today. "Yes. He is."

I saw an elderly couple facing the moment that had come to them. They could have easily wished for another time—to be young and tanning on a Florida vacation, to be raising two little girls in Kentucky, to be coming home from work, to be buying their new home in the prime of their careers. But these moments were gone and weren't coming back. A new moment waited for them, a moment beyond their control.

In this Lenten season, we wish for a time of our own choosing, of our own making. And our prayers are that God would make it be the time we want it to be. Ecclesiastes 3 is a wise reminder that life comes at us, times come and go, and we don't get to choose our seasons. We are temporary, fragile, mortal, dust-to-dust, ashes-to-ashes creatures. We can revolt against the reality of the time in which we find ourselves. But in so doing, we miss the presence of God in this moment. Only God can invade time. And the only time that God chooses to invade is this present moment.

I am reminded of the words that John uses to describe Jesus at the Last Supper table with his disciples. "Jesus knew that the hour had come . . ." (13:1). The Lenten journey invites us to accept what time it is for us.

Pray

Gracious God, grant us the capacity to fully accept the present moment that we live in. Deliver us from the illusion that we can wish ourselves into a different season. Grant us grace for this day, whatever it holds. And may we be aware that you are with us. Amen.

FIRST SUNDAY IN LENT

March 10, 2019

written by Dan Boone

Read

Luke 4:1–13

Additional: Deuteronomy 26:1–11 • Psalm 91:1–2, 9–16 • Romans 10:8b–13

Reflect

A friend recently gave me a book that I read years ago and had forgotten about: *In the Name of Jesus: Reflections on Christian Leadership*. The author, Henri J. M. Nouwen, was an early favorite of mine. I have several of his books, and it does me good to revisit them from time to time. *In the Name of Jesus* looks back on Nouwen's transition from a prestigious academic role at Harvard to working with the mentally impaired at the L'Arche communities in Toronto. The residents of the new community had high expectations regarding his presence among them. These expectations conflicted with his frequent travels as a speaker, so they decided that whenever he left the community to speak or lecture, one of the residents would accompany him. His reflections on Christian leadership are written in the context of studying the temptations of Jesus in his new community of mentally impaired friends with their expectations of his presence.

The first temptation of Jesus was to turn stones into bread. In a food desert, nothing could be more divinely relevant than using your own power to sustain and provide for yourself. A primary task of the Christian leader is to meet the needs of the people we serve. We are often tempted to sustain our own relevance by offering those we serve the things they want. It can be intoxicating to be the source of what people need, and it also contributes to job security. But Jesus resisted the temptation to be his own sustainer with the response that one does not live on bread alone. The full version of Jesus's response suggests that we live by the words of the Father, by listening to what God says. Jesus trusted that God would provide what he needed at the time he needed it.

The second temptation was power. The devil suggested that power over the kingdoms of the world was his to give to anyone he chose. Many have taken the devil up on his offer, and history is full of their destruction. Jesus, however, declined with the response, "Worship the Lord your God, and serve him only." While the devil's definition of leadership focused on getting people to do what we tell them to do, Jesus focused on doing what the Father told him. Jesus resisted leading and embraced being led.

The third temptation was to be spectacular: to leap from the pinnacle of the temple with the expectation that the Father would be true to Scripture and send angels to catch him before he split his feet on the stones below. Jesus responded by quoting part of a psalm: "Do not put the Lord your God to the test." Jesus exchanged the spectacular for the commonplace. He would fulfill his mission by serving people humbly rather than impressing them with religious showmanship. Rather than being the greatest show on earth, he would be the greatest servant on earth.

Nouwen closes the book by telling about his friend Bill, who accompanied him on a lecture given in Washington, DC, which Bill insisted they do together. He stood behind Nouwen as he lectured and stepped forward to turn the pages of his address. He interrupted Nouwen a few times to assure the listening crowd that he had witnessed what Henri was telling them. At the end, Bill asked for the privilege of adding his comments. His speech went like this: "Last time, when Henri went to Boston, he took John Smeltzer with him. This time he wanted me to come with him to Washington, and I am very glad to be here with you. Thank you very much." Bill's presence and impairment brought gifts to an otherwise stuffy lecture series in an expensive hotel located in the seat of global power. The way of God in the world is life-giving, playful, and creative. Maybe there is another way to live out the kingdom of God on earth: by exchanging self-sustenance for prayer, leading for being led, and the spectacular for commonplace service.

Pray

Gracious God, open us to the kind of leadership that we learn from Jesus. Amen.

MARCH 11, 2019

written by Dan Boone

Read

Psalm 17

Additional: 1 Chronicles 12:1–17 • 1 John 2:1–6

Reflect

Enemies are out there. They will hurt us if they can. At times they are cold and arrogant. They usually fight sideways or attack from the rear. Their goal is to shame, embarrass, discredit, or harm, and they will seize any available opportunity to do so. Their words are poison. Their compliments are backhanded. Our success is their worst nightmare. Our failure is their cherished dream. They can be shrewd, look civil, and pass for moral. They are often deeply angry, insecure, or afraid, but they don't know it. They come in all shapes and sizes. In the language of Psalm 17, "They close their hearts to pity; with their mouths they speak arrogantly. They track me down; now they surround me; they set their eyes to cast me to the ground. They are like a lion eager to tear, like a young lion lurking in ambush" (vv. 10–12, NRSV).

Enemies are out there. In Psalm 17, an enemy has struck. The psalmist opens his heart wide enough for us to watch him process his pain. He believes he has done nothing to deserve his fate. He even appeals to his own righteousness. "If you try my heart, if you visit me by night, if you test me, you will find no wickedness in me; my mouth does not transgress. As for what others do, by the word of your lips I have avoided the ways of the violent. My steps have held fast to your paths; my feet have not slipped" (vv. 3–5, NRSV).

One of the ways to read the Psalms is to place them on the lips of Jesus. This is not meant to disregard the thoroughly ancient Jewish context of trouble that births these prayers, nor is it to New Testamentize the Old Testament. But when we hear the very Jewish Jesus appealing to the Father by way of the Psalms, we understand how these prayers hoped for deliverance from suffering. Jesus prayed these prayers. This one, in particular, seems to flow appropriately from his life of purity and obedience. The weightiest thing it does is place one fully in the hands of God when injustice and oppression rain down. "Guard me as the apple of the eye; hide me in the shadow of your wings, from the wicked who despoil me, my deadly enemies who surround me" (vv. 8–9, NRSV).

This psalm is standard operating procedure for enemies. It is called a lament, and the writer is following the form to the letter. In a structured lament, you address God, you bring your complaint to God and tell God what your enemy did to you, and you call on God to save you from your enemy. Psalms of lament function as Enemy 101. When something horrible happens and our world is threatened, it is good to have a ritual response that requires no thought. There is no time for reflection. We just need to act. Ritual is a better reaction than rage. Keep it simple. Call on God, tell God, ask God to save you. The lament structure keeps us from going off half-cocked. Our friend the psalmist is following the form. Psalms 35 and 109 are other good examples.

In these psalms we hear the outpouring of raw emotion in response to injustice. This is how humans honestly feel when an enemy intentionally hurts us. It is a normal response to being deeply and repeatedly wronged. We get hurt. And, somehow, we believe this matters to God.

Our Psalm 17 friend suggests that the person who is harming him needs a bellyful of what is in store for him. While verse 14 may sound somewhat sympathetic at first glance, it is best to read it sarcastically: *may he get what is coming to him along with his children and their children.* But then the psalm ends with a sense of settledness. "As for me, I shall behold your face in righteousness; when I awake I shall be satisfied, beholding your likeness" (v. 15, NRSV).

If this is the pattern of Jesus in dealing with suffering, it is also meant to be the pattern of the followers of Jesus: put our enemies in the hands of God and trust God to do what is just, loving, and right. In the process, we are delivered from living enemy-centered lives, from the internal acid of revenge, and from a life of retaliation. Who knows? In God's hands, miracles happen. We may even come to love our enemy.

Pray

Gracious God, may our Lenten sojourn among enemies drive us to the same psalms that Jesus prayed, with the same trust and hope that your justice will ultimately prevail over all evil. Amen.

written by Dan Boone

Read

2 Peter 2:4–21

Additional: Psalm 17 • Zechariah 3:1–10

Reflect

This is one of the oddest texts in the Bible. Peter is dealing with false prophets, and the antidote seems to be the judgment of God. He uses two biblical stories to assure his readers that God is capable of judgment: the flood of Noah's day and the destruction of Sodom and Gomorrah by fire. Let's revisit Noah.

It was a whisper spoken in the privacy of a bedroom. The boy who had given his parents fits had become a man. He had rebelled, disobeyed, disrespected them. And now, with his recent violence, he had broken their hearts. His latest escapade had gone beyond broken rules. He had left bodies broken. And his parents were in their bedroom talking. The lights had long been off. Sleep was long past due. He was out there somewhere, still doing violence to people. And one parent whispered the words of anguished regret. "I wish we'd never had him." If the boy could have been standing there, overhearing the whisper of grieved parents, would it have made a difference?

That's the question we are faced with in the story of Noah. In this well-known, deeply loved story, we are brought face to face with the regret of God that results in judgment. We overhear God say, "I wish I'd never made them. I will destroy them with a flood." And God is talking about you and me.

Our story does not begin with regret. It begins with words like "and God saw . . . and it was good." God is pleased with his creation and his creatures. They stroll the garden and discuss horticulture and animal monikers. They share a common interest in work and play. They take the same break at the end of each week. They are partners in creation. God has made space in the universe for will to exist other than his own. They are free. They are empowered to cooperate with God in the management of the world. It is good. Very good.

But in Genesis 3, things begin to unravel in a very bad way. Eve sees something she wants and seizes it. Adam follows suit. Not satisfied with the partnership arrangement, they wish to be self-sustained, independent creatures. They will fend for themselves now that they know good and evil. They both run and hide. In hiding, they cover themselves from God and from each other. It is no longer safe to be naked in the world. Curses follow. Eve bears babies in pain. Adam farms fields in sweat. The ground grows weeds. And the worst is yet to come. Eve gives painful birth to two boys. One eventually murders the other. They have more babies. Evil multiplies exponentially across the earth. God's vision of a creation at rest is plunging faster than a roller coaster.

And before you know it, we hear this: "The Lord saw that the wickedness of humankind was great in the earth, and that every inclination of the thoughts of their hearts was only evil continually. And the Lord was sorry that he had made humankind on the earth, and it grieved him to his heart. So the Lord said, 'I will blot out from the earth the human beings I have created—people together with animals and creeping things and birds of the air, for I am sorry that I have made them'" (Gen. 6:5–7, NRSV).

We're on page 5 of a thousand-page story, and the main character is already having second thoughts. In five pages we've gone from "and God saw . . . and it was good" to "and God saw . . . and regretted." The grief in God's heart is the same word for the pain in the woman's womb. God's creatures are seeing and seizing. They are destroying the earth. Violence—or *hamas* in Hebrew—covers the earth.

I'd always thought of the story of Noah and the ark as a good story about animal pairs and rainbows in the sky. Not anymore. It is the story of the regret of God, a dark moment when God decides to wash creation away. As I read the text, it seems to suggest that, had God known in Genesis 1:1 what God knew in Genesis 6:5, he'd never have made us. Like the parents whispering in the bedroom, he wished we'd never been born.

If I were reading the Bible for the first time and came to the Noah story on page 5, I'd be thinking some serious thoughts about the characters. These humans really are free to destroy each other . . . and so is God. Only God is a lot better at blotting out.

The freedom of God is more frightening than the freedom of humans. God is on the verge of giving up his vision for a partnership. God is grieved deeply and regrets having ever made humanity. God is deciding to pull the plug on the universe. God is vulnerable to the evil we do. It gets to him. God can be pushed too far.

Pray

Gracious God, give us pause at the coldness that develops within us when we think you are incapable of responding to human evil with judgment. Save us from ourselves. Amen.

written by Dan Boone

Read

Job 1:1–22

Additional: Psalm 17 • Luke 21:34–22:6

Reflect

Sometime in your life you will probably suffer. Some great pain will flood your life with sorrow and agony. You will not understand why, and though you look for a reason, you will not find one. We are wired to want answers. It's why books about suffering become bestsellers: *When Bad Things Happen to Good People, Where Is God When it Hurts?, When God Doesn't Make Sense.*

Many of us who are followers of God wish there were simple answers because we've been cornered by doubters who nail us with their questions. How can a loving God let people be killed in gas ovens at Dachau? Why the Twin Towers, school shootings, and mass murder from a hotel balcony? And, much closer to home, what about Dave, and Josh, and Mary?

We cannot explain why. We float our guesses, but it doesn't stop the questions. Nor does God pipe in with help. There is an awkward silence. Suffering strips away the veneer of life. We learn that we are not as secure as we thought. We ask, "Why me?" Some of us go through our life with a fine-toothed comb looking for transgressions that could possibly make us deserving of such a blow. Suffering changes the way we see the world, and it shatters certain kinds of faith. We talk about God (or don't talk about God) in ways different from before.

Job understands. If you come to his story wanting simple answers, prepare to be disappointed. God does not explain himself. The God who is silent for most of the book will speak eventually, though not convincingly enough to settle the matter. There are still questions.

The people who live in New Orleans can tell you stories about the destructive power of water. A raging hurricane named Katrina collapsed dams, washed away levies, and overran sandbags. Every hedge of protection set up against the tide was futile. It took everything in its path and sent people in search of higher ground.

The people of Noah's day had no ground high enough, no safe places to which to flee. A flood became the instrument of God's judgment on their sin. God stepped aside and allowed chaos to do what it does best—destroy all living things. God removed the hedge of protection. That's what happened to Job too. A different kind of flood came crashing down on him.

The story begins with God bragging about Job: upright, blameless, devout, greatest man among the people of the East, a righteous man with a fully devoted heart, a man of integrity. This is Billy Graham, Mother Teresa, and Saint Francis of Assisi all rolled into one holy man. This is not just a nice guy; this is the most righteous man on all the earth.

Then Satan comes along and makes God a bet that God decides to accept. I'm not sure I'd want God betting on me. But God believes Job's righteousness is deeper than trinkets and treasures. God decides to give Job the terrible dignity of proving that his integrity runs deeper than what he gets from God. Right off the bat we are given to understand that God is not about utilitarian religion—that is, religion for reward. There is actually something satanic about serving God for what we can get. To serve God for reward, insurance, blessing, or a protective hedge is to fall short of knowing God as God wishes to be known. This makes God into an idol to be appeased for the goodies. God refuses to let such a claim stand.

Satan says Job is righteous only because God has built a hedge around him. So God removes the hedge. In our story, God is sovereign. Satan cannot operate without permission. God is free to do as God pleases without needing permission from anyone. God removes the hedge. God allows Job's suffering. The Old Testament man was correct in understanding that, ultimately, both good and evil can come from the hand of God—whether by cause or permission.

We've done our human best to protect ourselves from catastrophe: home security systems, insurance policies, neighborhood watch, health checkups, nest eggs, air bags, steel bars, passwords, identity protection, armed forces. And most of the time our hedges hold. We are mindful to have good, thick hedges. As Christians, we half believe that, if we serve God, our families will be protected and our homes secured from danger. We'd like to believe that being in church every week gives us a better chance at escaping calamity. But there are too many among us who have gotten the positive test back, who have buried children, lost jobs, had hearts broken. And we know that hedge religion is not foolproof. But we wish it were. And if it were, Satan would be right: we would do it for what we get back in return.

God removed the hedge around Job. And the Sabeans raided Job's oxen. Lightning struck Job's sheep and shepherds. The Chaldeans stole Job's camels. A tornado killed Job's children. In rapid-fire order he was reduced to nothing. His business: gone. His possessions: gone. His children: gone.

And yet, even in all his grief, Job's response is to praise the Lord. God is winning the wager. The hedge is gone, but Job has not cursed God. He grieves, yet he clings to his integrity. Be careful not to paint Job as stoic, though. Within a few chapters he will be questioning God, yelling at God, trying to sue God, and accusing God. But he never walks away from God. For now, he sits on the ash heap of social rejection with all the other failures and losers, the cursed folk.

Another biblical character whose name also begins with 'J' will suffer in a similar place. What form of righteousness will rise from this heap of ashes? Maybe Jesus will show us when we get to Jerusalem's cross.

Pray

Gracious God, grant us the faith of Job that is most fully understood in the faithfulness of Jesus as he suffers his way to a cross. Amen.

THURSDAY
MARCH 14, 2019

written by Dan Boone

Read

Philippians 3:2–12

Additional: Genesis 13:1–7, 14–18 • Psalm 27

Reflect

This text has my interest, as would any text that begins as descriptively as this one does. It sounds like a Zombie apocalypse warning about flesh-eating creatures on the rampage. And maybe it is. Paul is warning his Philippian friends that preachers will come hawking a gospel of salvation through circumcision. Given his background, Paul is well aware of the seductive lure of this promised path to salvation. He warns them that salvation is not something that can be granted or secured by a religious scalpel but, rather, through knowing Christ and the power of his resurrection.

As his primary example, Paul contrasts his flesh-based righteousness with his knowing-Christ righteousness. And if anyone has bragging rights regarding a righteousness based on human accomplishment, Paul would be the leader of the pack. He was raised in Jewish tradition, and he followed the letter of the

Jewish law, right up until Jesus confronted him on the road to Damascus and inspired his change of heart.

Lots of theological ink has been shed ridding us of legalistic self-righteousness. I have not actually met anyone lately who is so morally good that they stake a claim to saving grace based on their law-keeping prowess. Instead, I see the opposite. People don't take the law of God seriously at all. They neither study it nor obey it. Unlike John Wesley, who saw in every law a promise from God, today the law of God is seen as a burden or is used as a weapon for judging others. We are quick to defend ourselves when anyone suggests that the law of God might belong in the story of our redemption. Rather than being quick to believe that the law of God can be fulfilled in us by the indwelling Christ and the empowering Spirit, we seem to believe that human flesh is so corrupt, so tainted with sin, that nothing righteous is possible in these bodies of ours. We've moved away from a confidence-in-the-flesh legalism toward an everybody-sins-all-the-time expectation. I'm not sure this conclusion is where Paul was headed.

He goes on to write about the surpassing value of knowing Christ, gaining Christ, having a righteousness based on the faithfulness of Christ, sharing in the sufferings of Christ, and being made like Christ. Paul believes that Christ is the definition of what it means to be human. Our problem is not that we have wrongly achieved salvation via moral goodness but that we have underestimated what an intimate relationship with the faithful Jesus can mean. Paul was encountered by a Christ who was utterly transforming.

Isn't this interesting? We began this text with warnings about what false preachers (dogs, evildoers) want to do to our flesh (circumcision). We end the text in full assurance that the claim of Christ is on our fleshly bodies. Jesus Christ makes us his own. Jesus lays claim to these bodies of ours. We share in his sufferings in these bodies, and we will ultimately know him by the resurrection of these bodies. And this is the goal that drives us forward each day in fulfillment of our humanity. The bull's-eye of God's sanctifying intent lies in these bodies of ours. Paul wanted his friends in Philippi to see Christ living in him. Maybe that is what the world needs to see in us.

Pray

Gracious God, renew us in the likeness of your Son. May our bodies be your holy temple. Amen.

MARCH 15, 2019

written by Dan Boone

Read

Philippians 3:17–20

Additional: Genesis 14:17–24 • Psalm 27

Reflect

Yesterday, we saw Paul inviting his Philippian friends to know Christ in the way that he had come to know Christ. In so doing, they would be restored to their full humanity as those formed in likeness to Jesus. In this continuation of the text today, Paul invites them to imitate him. Few of us are bold enough to suggest that our friends pattern their lives after our own. Apparently, though, Paul was concerned about other role models in the community. Would his friends pattern their lives after these "enemies of the cross of Christ" who were posing as exemplary beacons of human thriving? After all, they were prestigious and successful in the cultural estimation of their day. They were the pretty people, the powerful people, the persuasive people of Philippi. Paul had already warned his friends about them. Whom they patterned their lives after mattered to Paul.

At the heart of the letter to the Philippians is the story of the crucified Christ. The letter takes the form of a typical friendship letter of this period, and it bears the personal concern of an imprisoned Paul for his friends. Were the enemies of the cross telling his dear friends, "Why would you want to follow Paul? Look what it got him. He's rotting in a Roman jail with a potential death sentence hanging over his head. He's traveled all over the world preaching the message of a crucified messianic figure and telling you that this is where life is. Really? You want to be that kind of loser? You want to pattern your life after a crucified criminal who was an enemy of the state and a two-bit preacher who is incarcerated? Who in their right mind wants to be a character in that sad story? Let us tell you how to really live! We have a much better story with a much better ending."

Paul knows the seductive power of competing narratives to claim human life. The dark stories of the world attempt to script us as characters in their plot. In essence, they are trying to assimilate us. Any *Star Trek* fans reading this? Remember the Borg? They were these part-human, part-machine creatures that possessed a common consciousness. They were made out of conquered peoples. Their mantra was "Resistance is futile; you will be assimilated." The enemies of the cross of Christ were the Borg of their day, seducing their fellow humans into a story that promised everything but delivered little that dignified humanity.

The Borg are alive and well in our world. I feel their power when I resist the dominating narrative that drives a consuming and conquesting culture. It is a downward pull of epic proportions. No wonder Paul wrote with tears as he warned his friends about the enemies of the cross and their enticing gospel of reality.

Along the Lenten road, we must recognize that there are dangerous stories afoot. These dark narratives are disguised as our salvation, our long-lost hope, our human quest. But in essence, they are evil. They destroy us. The Bible even has a word for their ways—sin. Of course, we don't say that word much anymore. It's like saying "bomb" on an airplane. It will make people uncomfortable and bring you under intense scrutiny.

Episcopal priest Barbara Brown Taylor writes in *Speaking of Sin*, "The days are long gone when most preachers can stand up in pulpits and name people's sins for them. They do not have that authority anymore. What they can do, I believe, is to describe the experience of sin and its aftermath so vividly that people can identify its presence in their own lives, not as a chronic source of guilt, nor as sure proof that they are inherently bad, but as the part of their individual and corporate lives that is crying out for change. . . . Sin is our only hope, because the recognition that something is wrong is the first step toward setting it right again. There is no help for those who admit no need of help. There is no repair for those who insist that nothing is broken."

Paul knows the message of the enemies of Christ and the outcome of following those enemies. He also knows the narrative of the crucified Jesus and offers himself as an example of this way. We are called to live as imitators of the crucified Jesus, daring to refute the competing narratives that destroy our friends.

Pray

Gracious God, on this Lenten journey may we be ever so bold as to suggest that people imitate us as we follow you. Maybe this will help us follow you more intentionally and speak of sin more clearly and love our friends more carefully. Amen.

SATURDAY
MARCH 16, 2019

written by Dan Boone

Read

Psalm 118:26–29

Additional: Psalm 27 • Matthew 23:37–39

Reflect

We recognize these words as the welcome offered to Jesus by the Jerusalem crowd at his triumphal entry into the city of David. Jesus comes humbly, riding on a donkey, people wave palm branches, they lay coats along the pathway, and they cheer the one who comes in the name of the Lord.

Psalm 118 is a song of victory. The Lord has heard and answered the cries of his people (vv. 5–9). The Lord has acted mightily (v. 16). The gates are opened for the coming of this saving God (vv. 19–20). The rejected stone has become the chief cornerstone (v. 22). This is a day for rejoicing (vv. 24–25). For all practical purposes, this psalm looks like a victory lap, somewhat similar to the Kansas City Royals parade following the final victory of the 2015 World Series. Finally, we win!

But what if the reign that God establishes with this king is radically different from the reign we want? What if this king is not about protecting our vested interests, or getting our party elected in the halls of Congress, or protecting our tribe from all the other tribes, or our national supremacy, or satisfying our consumptive lifestyles, or enhancing our brand, or securing our possessions? What if this king is coming to call for the surrender of our vested interests to a radically different agenda that is more about others than it is about us? What if this king views politics as humble service for the common good, rather than using one's power to champion the demands of those who paid the most? What if this king baptizes us into a new people with a new identity, rather than protecting our tribal wishes? What if this king does not care about putting America first or, even more unimaginable, suggests that the first shall be last? What if this king demands less consumption? What if the brand of this king is not wealth and jets and fame but a towel and a basin of water? What if this king demands lifelong generosity toward those who have less? What if the way of this king is suffering love rather than coercive power?

Will you still go the parade and declare this king, this way of life, this Jesus to be "the one who comes in the name of the Lord"? We tend to want a king who secures our tribe, our wants, and our place in the world or, if this is not possible, one who leads us in retreat from a world that won't give us what we want.

James K. A. Smith writes in *Awaiting the King*, "The call to follow Christ, the call to desire his kingdom, does not simplify our lives by segregating us in some 'pure' space; to the contrary, the call to bear Christ's image complicates our lives because it comes to us in the midst of our environments without releasing us from them. The call to discipleship complicates our lives precisely because it introduces a tension that will only be resolved eschatologically."

If we dare stand in the streets and shout Psalm 118, we will be people desiring a king and kingdom unlike anything this world has ever elected. But it is appropriate for us to do this—because this is the king and the kingdom that are en route even now.

Pray

Gracious God, grant us faith to welcome your future even though the kingdoms of this world cannot imagine it. And as we welcome your king to reign in us, may the watching world recognize that a revolution is underway. Amen.

SECOND SUNDAY IN LENT

March 17, 2019

written by Samantha Chambo

Read

Psalm 27

Additional: Genesis 15:1–12, 17–18 • Luke 9:28–43a
or Luke 13:31–35 • Philippians 3:17–4:1

Reflect

For what are you waiting? Are you waiting for a positive outcome
of a difficult situation, or are you waiting in anticipation for
something you desire? Whatever it may be, I am sure it can't be
easy. Waiting can be most challenging. In these days of instant
coffee, emails, and text messages we hardly have to wait for
anything anymore. Society has become more efficient and con-
cise, but the result is that human tolerance for waiting has gone
down significantly.

Some things just cannot be rushed, though, such as a response
from a prospective employer, a diagnosis from a doctor, or for
medicine to take effect. Other situations include a beloved teen-

ager who has to pass through a rebellious phase, a marriage in desperate need of healing, or the anguish of grief for a lost loved one that needs to subside. Waiting can be torture, but there is also a blessing in it.

Psalm 27 is about waiting. It is clear that there are many things that the psalmist needs, but he mentions the one thing he is expecting. He is waiting for the Lord. He knows the presence of God is sufficient to meet any need he might have. In the face of war, persecution, and rejection, he chooses to seek God; his only desire is to see the face of the God he loves, to live in the holy presence. The psalmist has full confidence that he can face anything that might come his way because he has the all-sufficient God on his side. God is even better than the love of a mother or father.

Waiting on God takes courage. Sometimes it just seems easier to look for a quick fix; other times, the process of waiting can inflict such pain that withdrawal from the process seems more reasonable. The opinions of others can be a significant obstacle while we wait on God. Reasonable people making logical suggestions can pressure us to give up on God and seek other avenues. Sometimes the people we love most compel us to abandon our post. Waiting on God can be a lonely process because people tend to withdraw when they think we are misguided. Another force to reckon with is the enemy within. Sometimes our fear and a desire for explanations and results can cause doubt in God's promises, and we find ourselves tempted to start looking for answers elsewhere. Waiting for the Lord can be hard.

The blessing for those who wait for God is that he is already present. We may not always see evidence of his presence, but we know he waits with us because he promised he would (Deut. 31:6). So, we wait in him, which means to consciously seek God during our waiting season, to depend on the help of the Holy Spirit to fortify us while we wait. We do this through prayer, praise, worship, meditation, and fasting. We seek the advice of spiritual people, and we serve humbly while we wait. Then one day we realize that the blessing of waiting is intimacy with Christ, who faithfully waits with us.

Another blessing is our transformation. Waiting in Christ can be a time of reflection on the holiness of Christ, which in turn reveals our shortcomings. Pride, the need for control, impatience, self-centeredness, envy, and other niggling traits come to light, providing opportunity for us to confess, repent, and become more like our Savior. As we wait, we are being changed into the beauty of Christ while we stare intently at his holiness (2 Cor. 3:18).

Pray

Lord, teach us to wait expectantly for you. We put our hope in you. Teach us to have the courage to wait patiently for your salvation. Amen.

MONDAY

MARCH 18, 2019

written by Samantha Chambo

Read

Exodus 33:1–6

Additional: Psalm 105:1–42 • Romans 4:1–12

Reflect

One aspect of God's character that still baffles Christians is his tendency to punish people for their sins. We try to avoid thinking about it because it scares us. We think of scenes from the Old Testament, where fire, floods, snakes, and other horrors were just a few methods used to bring punishment on humans. One comforting thing in all of these stories is that God's grace always prevails; his steadfast love always provides a second chance for wayward humans.

The scene in Exodus 32 and 33 is no different. Moses has been on Mount Sinai for a long time, where he was receiving the Ten Commandments from God. Meanwhile, at the foot of the mountain, the people convinced Aaron that Moses was not coming back and that they needed a new god. So Aaron took all their jewelry and made a golden calf. When Moses descends the mountain, he is greeted by the shocking scene of people dancing, reveling, and worshiping this golden calf. Moses is so shocked that he throws down the stone tablets, shattering them. God in his anger brings severe punishment on the people, and many of them die. But the worst punishment is when God declares he will not go up to the promised land with them; instead, he will instead send an angel to accompany them.

This awful scene also became the place of the most intimate and loving interaction between God and humans. The people started to mourn because of their sins and stripped themselves of all ornaments as a sign of their repentance. Moses begged God to go with them, explaining that they were nothing without their God, and he pleaded for the physical manifestation of God's holy presence. Here in the ashes of the worst human failure, we see the results of real repentance. God assured them of his presence, even making a physical appearance wherein Moses could see his back, and the glory of the Lord shone from Moses's face for many days after, but the best part was that God went with them. He did not leave them to their own devices but continued to guide them to the promised land.

God's continued presence and his continued grace in spite of human failure are evidence of his steadfast love. The most conclusive proof is that God sent his Son, Jesus, to come and live among us and be with us. Jesus also took the punishment for our sins on himself when he died on the cross. He won the victory over sin and death when he was raised from the dead, enabling us to live lives that please God. He gave us his Holy Spirit to be in us and with us. God never leaves us to our own devices. He is always present, making way for our salvation and deliverance. The whole Bible tells this story: God loves us, never leaves us, and is always making way for our restoration to himself.

Human beings will never be able to understand the full complexity of the divine nature. However, we know all we need to know: God loves us so much that he sent his Son to die for our sins (John 3:16). He is always near and willing to save us when we ask.

Pray

Father, we thank you for your steadfast love. Thank you that you have made way for our salvation through Jesus Christ. Teach us your ways so we can live lives that please you. Amen.

Read

1 Corinthians 10:1–13

Additional: Numbers 14:10b–24 • Psalm 105:1–42

Reflect

Paul wrote these words to the members of the Corinthian church, who found themselves in a tight spot. They had to decide whether it was right to eat food that had been offered to idols (1 Cor. 8–10). It seems like a straightforward problem for us, but it was more complicated for the churches in Corinth. Idol worship was the norm. Everyone in society participated in feasts for the gods, and sacrifices to the gods were made at every social and political event. People even dedicated their meals at home to the gods, so these new Christians would be faced with this problem if they went to visit an unsaved friend. Not eating food offered to idols meant they would have to exclude themselves from social events, and for many of them, social status was desired. Some of them were poor, and sometimes the only meat they could afford was the meat sold by the temple priest in the open market after it had been offered to the gods. So believers tried to rationalize, saying that these gods were not real, so it didn't matter if they ate meat that had been offered to idols.

But Paul cautioned them that they should not be deceived so easily. He said that eating food sacrificed to idols could cause those who were weak in faith to fall back into sin, that eating food offered to idols meant sharing a table with demons. Most importantly, in chapter 10, he assured them that eating idol food was a form of idol worship and that they should flee from it. Paul used examples from the history of Israel to warn them that idolatry had serious consequences. Paul knew he was asking something challenging from the Corinthians. That is why he gave them this assurance: *you can do this because God himself will help you overcome the temptation.*

Paul describes idolatry as "setting our hearts on evil things" (10:6). For the Corinthians, this "evil thing" was the need for social status and acceptance by unbelievers. These days there are many things we are tempted to set our hearts on instead of God. Money, status, success, another human being, and the list can be endless. Those things tempt us to be disobedient to God because we want them so badly. However, we have the assurance that there is no temptation we cannot overcome. God, in his faithfulness, will provide an escape. But we have to be willing to be obedient when the Holy Spirit directs us away from the temptation.

The starting point is to identify the things on which we have set our hearts. We need to ask the Holy Spirit to show us the areas of our hearts that are divided. These are the things we think about most of the time, the things we spend our time, money, and energy on. Things that prompt us to tell the white lie, or turn a blind eye when needed. It can be things that cause shame, that we tend to hide from others, that bring a wedge between us and our loving Father. Once we have identified the main desire, adverse actions can be identified, and we can pray for deliverance as we walk in daily obedience. Victory over temptation is possible because Christ already assured our success when he rose from the dead. We can overcome anything when we are in Christ.

Pray

Father, thank you for your faithfulness. Search our hearts and reveal to us any areas of idolatry. Help us to live in the victory that Christ Jesus won for us on the cross. Amen.

written by Samantha Chambo

Read

Luke 13:22–31

Additional: 2 Chronicles 20:1–22 • Psalm 105:1–42

Reflect

We all want to be included. Such a desire is only human. And, if possible, we want to be one of the first to be chosen, like when we used to play games as children. The ones who were picked last felt rejected and hurt. So the natural response, when faced with any new social situation, is to find out what the requirements are for inclusion. When it comes to inclusion in the kingdom of Christ, the stakes are even higher, except the usual rules are turned upside down.

Jesus tells a heart-wrenching parable in today's scripture. He describes a scenario where multitudes of people are waiting at a narrow door to enter to a great feast. Many are allowed to enter, from all the corners of the world, but many are also left outside to view the festivities through the window. The most disturbing detail is that those left out are those we would expect to be admitted. These are the people who ate and drank and were familiar with the host, but he will not open for them, saying he does not know them. Those left outside start to weep in despair, but they also get angry when they see lowly people sitting in what they expected to be their seats, so they gnash their teeth in frustration. Jesus then ends the parable by saying that the first will be last and the last will be first.

This parable disturbs us because it raises the question of who will finally make it into Christ's glorious kingdom in heaven. The Jews listening to Jesus believe they have automatic inclusion because they are the children of Abraham. But Jesus tells them that this is not the case. Only those who strive to enter the narrow door will be admitted.

"The narrow door" is a term packed with meaning. In John 10:9, Jesus refers to himself as the gate, saying that entrance into his kingdom is only by faith in him. The narrow gate also has another significance to the Jews. They know the synagogue has two doors, a wide one and a narrow one. The wide door is used by the important people like the high priest and the wealthy. The poor, the sick, and the marginalized have to use the narrow door to gain entrance into the synagogue. In comparing entrance into the kingdom of God with a narrow door, Christ makes humility and identification with the marginalized important requirements to enter the kingdom of God. Jesus is letting the religious teachers know that they will only be admitted if they have faith that he is the Savior of the world and if they humble themselves and identify with the marginalized in society.

Jesus tells them to "strive" to enter (NRSV). The word *strive* means to agonize; it is the word used for athletes who work very hard to prepare for a contest. This does not mean we get into heaven by our good works. It means the kingdom of Christ must become our sole passion, the most essential aspect in our lives. It is more than just confessing faith in Jesus Christ and becoming a child of God. It requires a life driven by a passion to see the kingdom of Christ manifested in all the universe. These are the people who will be admitted.

Pray

Jesus, thank you for making a way for us to enter your glorious kingdom. Help us, by the power of your Holy Spirit, to make your kingdom the most important driving force of our lives. Amen.

THURSDAY
MARCH 21, 2019

written by Samantha Chambo

Read

Psalm 63:1–8

Additional: Daniel 3:19–30 • Revelation 2:8–11

Reflect

Desire has become the new buzzword among motivational speakers, life coaches, and psychologists. Neuroscience is beginning to prove that desire for anticipated reward is a powerful motivator for action. This means that the presence or lack of desire can affect how we live our lives. We go after the things we desire. Psalm 63 is a compelling picture of what happens when God is our primary desire.

The psalmist compares his desire for God to the thirst one feels after being stranded in the desert. So intense is his desire that he longs for God with his whole being. This overwhelming desire affects his actions. He seeks God; he goes up to the sanctuary to enjoy the beauty of God; he spends his time praising and giving glory to God. God is his primary desire; therefore, only God can satisfy him. He says the satisfaction is like the feeling of having had a rich meal—literally, after eating the fat and marrow, the most satisfying portions of meat. So consuming is his desire for

God that it fuels his whole day. He seeks God early in the morning and continues to remember God when he goes to bed and all through the night. He finds shelter in God's loving presence and clings to God for dear life.

This must be the desire Jesus was referring to when he said we must "love the Lord your God with all your heart and with all your soul and with all your strength and with all your mind" (Luke 10:27). To love like this is to desire God with one's entire being. When we love Christ in this manner, it will affect our thoughts, our actions, our entire way of life. It will be the dominating force that guides our day from the moment we wake up to the time we lay our heads on our pillows at night. Our desire for Christ must become the driving force of our lives, the one thing that brings true satisfaction to our souls. This is the ideal for those who stand in a relationship with Jesus.

However, the reality can sometimes be very far removed from the ideal. There are so many things that vie for our desires. Vendors who prey on our fragile desires for financial gain are always offering something new. The world and its value system try to prescribe to us what we ought to desire, and when we don't comply with the norm, we can be excluded. Then there is also human nature to contend with. We want the things that will make us look good, feel comfortable, and enjoy our lives. This can make it difficult to keep our desire focused on Christ.

Can we control what we desire? How can we make sure that our desire for Christ and his kingdom is more than just mere lip service? What do we do when the Holy Spirit reveals to us that our most basic desires are misplaced on the things of this world instead of Christ? The answer is simple. We ask God to change our desires because the Bible assures us that he will. Philippians 2:13 says "it is God who works in you to will and to act in order to fulfill his good purpose," and according to Romans 5:5, "God's love has been abundantly poured out within our hearts through the Holy Spirit who was given to us" (AMP). This is cause for great hope and joy for us. Christ, by his Holy Spirit, can fix our wrong desires and direct us toward our loving Father.

All we need to do is ask, and ask continuously, until we, like the psalmist, desire God with our entire beings.

Jesus, forgive us for our misguided desires. We pray that you, by your Holy Spirit, would direct our hearts toward you, that we might love you with our entire beings. Amen.

MARCH 22, 2019

written by Samantha Chambo

Read

Revelation 3:1–6

Additional: Psalm 63:1–8 • Daniel 12:1–4

Reflect

"I am well, thank you." This is a fib often told by people when asked how they are. There are many reasons people respond in this manner; they might feel that the person asking is not actually interested, or maybe they just prefer to keep up appearances. This can also be the case with our spiritual well-being. There are times when we do all the right things, attend all the church programs, and say all the correct words, but deep down we are like the church in Sardis. We know we are dying spiritually, but we prefer to keep up the pretense.

The church in Sardis was doing well by all appearances. They had a good reputation of being alive. However, they could not fool Christ, who accused them of being dead. The church in Sardis became secularized, taking on the norms and behaviors of the inhabitants around them. As a result, they were not persecuted like some of the other churches mentioned in Revelation. Jesus said their works were incomplete and that they were no longer evangelizing the city; instead, they were conforming. In short, they had become nominal Christians, having a form of godliness without any spiritual power (2 Tim. 3:5). The Christians in Sardis bore the name Christian, but they were too lethargic to live the life that was required of them.

Jesus made a desperate plea that they wake up and remember the gospel they received and the life they lived when they first became Christians. The warning is urgent because Jesus would return soon, this time as a judge, and those who did not repent would suffer eternal death, while those who chose to remain in Christ would be rewarded with entrance into the Father's kingdom.

This warning to the church in Sardis still rings true today. We need to be vigilant. Otherwise, we might find ourselves half dead and unprepared for the return of Christ. The city of Sardis had experience with the result of a lack of vigilance. Sardis was built on a mountain, which made it almost impossible to be invaded. However, it was invaded twice when the city let down its guard. We need to treasure our spiritual life and be watchful, lest we are lulled into spiritual lethargy.

What do we do when we realize we have fallen asleep? Jesus says wake up and repent. This repentance is more than just confessing sin; it includes doing things differently. It means completing the things we have left half done; it means living as Christians even if it results in persecution.

We are to remember what we have received and heard. What did we receive and hear? We received the good news of Jesus Christ, who loved us so much that he gave his own life to save ours and is even now sitting at the right hand of the Father, interceding for us. This is the same passion exhibited in the life of Christ that must be reflected in our daily lives. A gospel such as this demands our wholehearted surrender; nothing less will do.

Pray

Jesus, search us today and reveal our spiritual condition. Forgive us for being lulled into a false sense of comfort. Stir up your Spirit in us and bring us back to life. Amen.

Read

Luke 6:43–45

Additional: Psalm 63:1–8 • Isaiah 5:1–7

Reflect

What are the things we store up in our hearts? What are the events and words and people that we save in the recesses of our inner person? According to Luke, these things determine how we relate to the world around us. Will we bring forth good fruit from the good that is stored up in our hearts, or will we sprout evil?

Every day of our lives is filled with people, events, and words that we can either store up in our memory or discard as trash. Some of the things we are confronted with are outside of our control, such as the environment and people we are faced with on a daily basis. However, some of the things we gather intentionally for our storeroom, such as the recreational activities we feel will add value to our lives, the media we focus on, and the people we choose to spend time with. Even in our interactions with people, we choose what to store up. People are fallible, so in one day they might give you a range of things to choose from. One person might come in and give you a muffin she baked, but later she might snap at you for a mistake you made. This again presents the question: What will you store up in your heart?

The word used in verse 45 is *thesauros*, meaning a repository, treasure, the things seen to be of value and kept for safekeeping. Luke 2:19 says Mary kept all the events surrounding the birth of Jesus in her heart. She treasured in her heart the words of the angels, the coming of the shepherds and the wise men, and all the marvelous things she was allowed to experience by the grace of God. Mary chose to treasure the good things, and the result was that she did not doubt who Jesus was, as proven with the first miracle at the wedding in Cana (John 2:1–11).

We cannot hide the things we have stored up in our hearts. In the same way, a tree cannot hide its true identity. It will always be revealed by the fruit it produces. This principle applies to humans as well. Unforgiveness, bitterness, envy, and strife will gush out of us sooner or later if those are what we tend to store up in our hearts. The opposite is true as well. When we choose to see the good in people and remember the good times more than the bad; if we select carefully whom we will allow to speak into our lives, and what media we will consume; if we choose to think about others in a grace-filled way and allow for human weakness, the resulting fruit will not be concealed. It will be like a good tree, giving life and joy to those who gather in its shade.

We might have collected the contents for our hearts unconsciously up to this point, but we can always choose to be more intentional about it going forward. We can choose to store up the excellent and holy and praiseworthy things, and in return, we will be a source of good to the world around us.

Pray

Father, up to this point maybe we haven't paid much attention to all that we have stored up in our hearts. Reveal to us the evil that does not belong and cleanse us thereof. Fill us with your love and grace, and give us the courage to choose the contents of our store with intentionality in the future. Amen.

THIRD SUNDAY IN LENT

March 24, 2019

written by Samantha Chambo

Read

Luke 13:1–9

Additional: Psalm 63:1–8 • Isaiah 55:1–9 • 1 Corinthians 10:1–13

Reflect

Repentance is a familiar refrain among church people. Unfortunately, it has lost a lot of its meaning over time. These days, repentance means feeling sorry for your sin and confessing both your sin and your sorrow over it to God in your prayer time. Although this is part of the definition of repentance, it also means so much more.

Repentance is one of the leading ideas in the Gospel of Luke. Jesus calls his listeners to repent not only as individuals but also together, as the people of God. Repentance in the New Testament means to feel remorse, to feel pain, to change one's mind. It signifies a turning away from sin and toward God. Repentance means to change one's very way of life. This meaning is clear

when John the Baptist says, "Produce fruit in keeping with repentance" (Matt. 3:8). There can be no doubt concerning true repentance because the drastic change in behavior will be obvious.

In Luke 13 Jesus first calls his listeners to personal repentance.
He urges them not to think of the sins of the Galileans they
question him about, but to instead focus on their own sins and
repentance. Otherwise their fate will be worse than the people
mentioned. They will suffer eternal death. This was a plea to
every person listening to Jesus that day. Jesus warns that the
coming judgment is real and that they need to make sure they
are ready for that day.

In the parable of the fig tree and the vineyard, Jesus changes the
focus from the individual to the group. Any good Jew would be
aware of the prophecies in Isaiah 5:2 and Jeremiah 8:13, where
God refers to the nation of Israel as a fig tree and a vine. These
prophecies express the anguish over their calloused hearts
and warn that lack of repentance would lead to judgment. This
makes the responsibility of repentance even greater.

We have a mandate to call our generation to repentance. We
must be the prophetic voice that calls the church of Christ away
from conformity to the world and toward a life that has a radical
impact on the world around us. However, this can be difficult
because those we admonish might perceive us as judgmental.
That should not stop us from urging our loved ones toward
repentance.

Jesus warns that the time for repentance is not infinite. In the
parable, the gardener begs that the tree be given one more year
to start bearing fruit. However, concerning the return of Christ,
no one knows the day or the hour he will return, which makes
repentance an urgent matter.

Sometimes we are convicted of our need for repentance, but we
put it off because we want to enjoy our sin just a little longer.
Failure to repent can lead to spiritual death and eternal separa-
tion from Christ. However, we can rejoice because Jesus gave his

life so that no one has to die, and he is working by his Spirit to move us to true repentance: repentance that leads to a church that makes an impact on the world for the sake of Christ.

Pray

Father, thank you for your patience with us. Help us as your church to turn from our sinful ways and embrace the life of holiness that you have provided for us. Amen.

MARCH 25, 2019

written by Samantha Chambo

Read

Romans 2:1–11

Additional: Psalm 39 • Jeremiah 11:1–17

Reflect

It's amazing how quick we are to make judgments on the behavior of others, while we always seem to find ways to justify our own sinful behaviour. We call our anger righteous and our lack of forgiveness justified, but we have little tolerance for the weakness of others. The weakness of others should be an incentive to cling even harder to the cross of Christ because we know that we are who we are because of God's grace; we have nothing to boast about.

The wrath and the judgment of God are real. We'd rather focus on the love and grace of God because those seem less threatening. But we do have to be careful not to lose sight that the day is coming when we will all be judged according to the lives we have lived, and we will also be rewarded accordingly. This reality should motivate us to continually live humbly before Christ, always ready to confess, repent, and obey. We can live holy lives by the power of the Spirit of God in us.

Romans 2 is a continuation of chapter 1, where Paul mentions some of the things that provoke the wrath of God. Maybe we should take some time to reflect quietly on each one of these sins, praying for the Holy Spirit to reveal any wrongdoing in us. First, they did not glorify God as God (1:21). *Does Christ have total reign in my life, or do I still prefer to be in control?* They indulged in sexual immorality (v. 24). *Is there any sexual immorality in my thoughts and behaviors?* They worshiped created things instead of the living God (v. 25). *Am I in any way guilty of idolatry?* They were guilty of greed, envy, murder, insolence, arrogance, boasting, disobeying earthly parents, infidelity, lovelessness, and showing no mercy. They also approved these negative behaviors in others (vv. 29–32). *Am I guilty of any of these sins?* Is the Holy Spirit highlighting anything you need to confess? Let us confess our sins. Refuse to make excuses, and receive forgiveness with joy.

Becoming aware of our sins can lead to distress and hopelessness, but Jesus said that those who mourn because of their sins are blessed because they will be forgiven. We should embrace our distress over our sins because it is a sign of the Holy Spirit working in us to purify us.

The next step is to believe that Jesus can cleanse us of our sins and put us back into right relationship with God. We must receive the forgiveness offered by Christ and choose to avoid the previous lifestyle with the help of the Holy Spirit.

We know that God only reveals our sins to us because he loves us. We accept the freedom given to us by the Spirit of God. Once we receive and live in the freedom provided for us by the Holy Spirit through Christ Jesus, we will not need to make any more excuses for our sins. The wrath and the judgment of God are a reality, but those who live as the redeemed of Christ on a daily basis have no reason to worry.

Pray

Jesus, thank you for revealing our sins to us. We pray for the cleansing by the power of the Holy Spirit and the grace to live in the victory you have provided for us. Amen.

Read

Psalm 39

Additional: Ezekiel 17:1–10 • Romans 2:12–16

Reflect

The sudden, tragic loss of life has the power to cause most people to stop and evaluate their lives. This effect is even more difficult if the deceased was relatively young, a close friend or relative, and if the death happened unexpectedly. In these moments we become, like the psalmist, aware of our humanity and fragility. We realize anew that life is short, and like the psalmist, we ask the question "What do I look for? What is my purpose in life?"

Psalm 39 is a psalm of personal lament. The psalmist is experiencing some suffering, which leads to him taking a vow of silence as he prays and meditates and waits for God's deliverance. He chooses to speak to God about the dilemma he faces, and as he converses with God, he becomes aware of how insignificant humans are in comparison to God, how short and fragile human life and wisdom are. So he turns to God in desperation; he prays for deliverance and for the opportunity to taste joy once again while he is alive. He describes human life as a handbreadth, a mere breath, and humans as phantoms; he goes so far as to classify human exploits as vanity. These metaphors underline the fact that our time here on earth is limited, which is why we need a revelation from God about how we choose to spend this time. We do not need to know when we will die; rather, we need a call from God to teach us to value our time in the body. Are we spending our minutes and days on the things that matter most?

The psalmist asks God to let him know how fleeting his life is. This should be the prayer of every Christian. How would we live if we lived in the full awareness that our lives are short? What would we do differently? Satan lulls Christians into a false sense of security, and the result is that we disregard eternal matters for the sake of trivial ones. Living with the awareness of the eternal will help us enjoy the blessings God has provided for us, but it will also make us careful to prioritize the mission of Christ.

God is always trying to direct our attention back to him. Sometimes he has to rebuke and discipline "us for our good, in order that we may share in his holiness" (Heb. 12:10). The correct response to the discipline of God is to endure it and to change as the Holy Spirit directs. This response will prepare us for eternity with God.

The wonder of life in Christ is that we don't have to wait for his second coming to enjoy eternal blessings. The love, peace, and joy of the Holy Trinity are available to us in this life. We can enjoy these blessing when we put earthly things in their proper place—that is, behind the priorities of the kingdom of Christ.

Pray

Father, show us how fleeting our lives are, and help us to live every minute of them for your glory. Amen.

MARCH 27, 2019

written by Samantha Chambo

Read

Luke 13:18–21

Additional: Numbers 13:17–27 • Psalm 39

Reflect

The kingdom of Christ is transforming power. Whether it enters the life of a single person or a community or the world, it results in dynamic change.

Jesus compared the kingdom of God to a mustard seed and explains that, although a mustard seed is very small, it grows into a big tree that provides shade for everyone. Luke chooses to focus on the fact that the birds come to enjoy the branches, which points to all the people of all the nations who will benefit from the kingdom of God.

Jesus also compared the kingdom of God to yeast that a woman put in some flour. The yeast worked through the dough. This metaphor points to the infectious power of the gospel to transform those who choose to be part of the kingdom.

The kingdom of God is not just heaven and the hereafter; it includes the sovereign rule of God in this era and in the whole created world. It can be deceptive in that it appears to be small and insignificant, but the reality is that it is taking root and advancing fast. All of humanity is involved in the kingdom of Christ. Some are rejecting the kingdom and reserving judgment for themselves, and others are participating in the kingdom, sharing in its joys and advancing it to the world.

The two metaphors Jesus used to describe the kingdom point to the progressive nature of the kingdom. In the life of an individual, it should be like yeast, permeating every part of our beings, making us more like Christ. This should result in Christians who are so filled with the Spirit of God that they become a shade, a safe place for restless souls to find help. These believers also become a force to be reckoned with because they are always advancing the agenda of the kingdom, always working to prepare the way for the King of Kings and Lord of Lords. This is the kingdom life: we are being transformed by the Holy Spirit, and we are a force of transformation to the world around us. The kingdom is also progressive in the world. Christ is moving all of history toward his second coming.

The transformation of the kingdom does not only refer to the holiness of the church but also to the impact that the kingdom should have on society. As the followers of Christ increase, there is an expectation that societies should become more just and equitable. The widows, orphans, and elderly should be cared for. Refugees and foreigners should find a home. Corruption, exploitation, and marginalization should decrease as the yeast of the kingdom permeates all that comes into contact with it.

As ambassadors of the kingdom, we bring the kingdom of Christ wherever we find ourselves—always willing to suffer, sacrifice, and serve as we bring glory to God. Jesus is our example of what it means to be a kingdom citizen. The kingdom was his passion, and he gave all to make sure everyone has access to it. Living a kingdom life can lead to persecution because the kingdom of Christ is directly opposed to the kingdoms of the world. But

Christians take courage because they know that Christ has won the ultimate victory.

Pray

Our Father in heaven, may your kingdom come and your will be done on earth as it is in heaven. Make us ready to be agents for the advancement of your kingdom here on earth. Amen.

THURSDAY
MARCH 28, 2019

written by Samantha Chambo

Read

2 Corinthians 4:16–5:5

Additional: Joshua 4:1–13 • Psalm 32

Reflect

Sickness, aging, and death are some of the most difficult realities of life. They remind us that our stay on earth is temporary and that Christ has prepared an eternal place for us in heaven.

Paul knew too well about the burden that comes with aging and physical affliction. He also had his fair share of persecution and suffering. Everything he went through served to remind him that life in this body is temporary. Paul, who was himself a tent maker, compares life in the body to a tent. It might last sixty or eighty years, but it is temporary. This life, when compared to the span of eternity, goes by in the blink of an eye.

The eternal perspective helped Paul as he thought about the suffering he was still experiencing. It is just a moment when compared to eternity with Christ. This perspective encouraged him to fix his eyes on the unseen, the promises of God, and the hope he had for eternal life in Christ. He believed that Christ is not only preparing a beautiful heavenly dwelling for his people but also that he will give new, glorious bodies to those who have died in him. These bodies will be similar to the body Christ had after he rose from the dead (1 Cor. 15). These new bodies will be our eternal dwellings. So in the meantime, while we're waiting to be united with Christ eternally, either through death or his second coming, we hold on to the promises of our Savior.

The Holy Spirit of God, which is in us and with us, is the deposit, or down payment, that guarantees these promises. The Spirit testifies with our spirit that we are God's children, and he is also the manifestation of Christ's power in our lives on a daily basis (Rom. 8:11, 16).

Although the blessing is eternal, it has already started in those who love Christ. We are already renewed day by day (2 Cor. 4:16). This renewal is done by God himself through the power of his Holy Spirit. As our outer bodies become weaker and frail in age, our spirit is already being changed into its glorious, eternal outcome. We are being made new every day. So, as we face hardship, persecution, and physical challenges, we can rejoice every day because we are being made more like Christ. This is why Paul can say "we do not lose heart" (v. 16). We don't give up; we keep on working for Christ because we can see what is important in life—not the things that make our flesh feel good or that stroke our egos but the things that will add eternal value to our lives.

This blessed hope can be a source of great relief to us; it means we no longer have to keep up with worldly values. It is also a source of great inspiration and motivation. We cling to the hope that we will be changed into his glory, death will be swallowed up in victory, and we will enjoy the pleasure of his holy presence for all eternity (1 Cor. 15:51-54).

Pray

Jesus, help us to focus on what is unseen, on the things that matter. Help us live our lives according to eternal priorities. Amen.

MARCH 29, 2019

written by Samantha Chambo

Read

2 Corinthians 5:6–15

Additional: Joshua 4:14–24 • Psalm 32

Reflect

What motivates you to share the love of Christ to those around you? Paul advises that the love of God compels his followers to spread the gospel. The word *compel* means to urge so strongly that it can cause someone to be distressed. So this desire, this love in us is so strong that it creates distress in us. It means we can't sit still, we can't keep quiet; we must go, we must speak, we must serve. This love inside us is like a force that makes everything else fade and become rubbish. We have one driving force, and that is to share this love of Christ with the world.

However, it is not our love for Christ that Paul is referring to in this passage. Rather, it is the actual love *of* Christ (see v. 14). It is the love that was demonstrated when the holy Son of God came and suffered a most humiliating death on the cross. This is the love that Paul talks about, the greatest love of all. When we understand the height and depth and width of this love, then we are compelled, we are in distress, we are moved by an inner force to spread this love.

When we are convinced by the all-surpassing love of Christ, we take up the ministry of reconciliation. All of us were sinners; we were separated from God. But Christ gave his life in exchange for ours. The hostility that is a result of sin can come to an end because of the sacrificial death of Christ. This is why we work to give others the same blessings. We no longer live for ourselves. We live for him who died for us (v. 15). We give up our wants, our desires, our comforts. Everything else becomes insignificant in the light of Christ.

We work so that sinners who were far away from God can be brought back to God. We must live as examples of reconciliation. God is reconciling the world to himself, and we get to be part of that. We take courage because we know God is doing all that he promised he would do. God trusts us with the ministry of reconciliation. We work both on behalf of Christ and also in place of Christ. Christ becomes present when his servants enter the room. We not only speak on behalf of Christ, but our entire lives also represent Christ. When people see us, they see Christ.

Serving Christ is desire; it is love burning inside of us, driving us to participate in God's work of reconciling the world to himself, to bring about his new creation. Being a servant of Christ means that we no longer live for ourselves but for him who loved us and gave himself for us.

Pray

Jesus, fill us with your holy love, that we may be compelled to share it with those around us. Give us grace so that we can live as worthy ambassadors of your kingdom. Amen.

MARCH 30, 2019

written by Samantha Chambo

Read

Psalm 32

Additional: Exodus 32:7–14 • Luke 15:1–10

Reflect

Some of the most powerful weapons that Satan uses against believers are silence and secrets. We are so ashamed of our sinful thoughts or behaviors that we keep them a secret, which can lead to even greater spiritual distress.

Psalm 32 teaches us about the blessing found in the confession of sins, comparing those whose sins are forgiven to those who choose to hide their sin. The people who choose to confess are blessed, happy, and fortunate, but those who keep quiet are faced with great suffering. The psalmist says that keeping silent came at great cost to him. His bones wasted away, he found himself groaning all day and night, and he was drained of all his strength. This description depicts tremendous inner turmoil. The burden of silence became too much to bear.

Unfortunately, this is the situation of many Christians who are burdened by sin. Their secret sins become a life-sapping force that alienates them from God and other believers. Not confessing also traps us in a cycle of continuing to sin, while confession forces us to seek accountability and thus to turn our backs on sin. Sometimes these secrets not only trap us but other people who are also involved, thus creating a web of sin and lies that can become overwhelming.

David, who might be the author of this psalm, knows all about this. He sinned with Bathsheba (2 Sam. 11), and then, to cover his sins, he arranged for the murder of her husband, Uriah. He did find relief for his guilt when the prophet Nathan confronted him about his sin. David admitted his sin and was able to find freedom. This did not exempt him from punishment, though— the child he conceived with Bathsheba died. However, David rejoiced in knowing that his relationship with God was restored.

Confessing does not exempt us from the consequences of our sins, but it does offer a path to freedom and deliverance. It restores our relationship with God and allows us to live in the blessing of the provision made on the cross for us by Jesus Christ. We should not be like a mule that needs to be forced to do the right things. The sooner we turn to Christ, the sooner healing and restoration can begin in our lives.

We can come with confidence to Christ, irrespective of our sins because he promised that all who confess would be received and their sins forgiven (see 1 John 1:9). The extent of the confession depends on the situation we find ourselves in. Sometimes confessing to Christ in the privacy of our quiet time is sufficient. However, there are times when it is necessary to confess to others. These situations include when our sins have been harmful to others or when we are trapped in addictive behaviors. Confessing to a mature, Christ-loving Christian can help with our recovery. Sometimes we also need to ask for forgiveness from those whom we have hurt, and other times we need to make amends for harm we have caused. We can depend on the guidance of the Holy Spirit as we seek prayerfully how to deal with our individual problems.

The psalmist describes the blessed state of those whose sins are forgiven. He says they are protected by God and have the guidance of the highest counsel. Those whose sins are forgiven are surrounded by the unfailing love of God, and their lives are filled with joy.

The choice is ours. Will we continue to live in our secret sins, or will we accept the freedom and healing that come with confession?

Pray

Father, please give us the courage to confess and repent from hidden sin. Thank you that you will never turn us away when we seek you with all our hearts. Amen.

FOURTH SUNDAY IN LENT

March 31, 2019

written by Tara Beth Leach

Read

Luke 15:1–3, 11b–32

Additional: Joshua 5:9–12 • Psalm 32 • 2 Corinthians 5:16–21

Reflect

In our Gospel text, Jesus is once again accused of being too friendly with and too loving toward sinners and those considered to be outside the boundaries of the people of God. Jesus responds to his naysayers with a story to expand their imaginations. The parable of the prodigal son not only makes Jesus's naysayers uncomfortable, but perhaps it makes some of us uncomfortable too.

In the story of the prodigal son, the love of God is made visible not only in the heart and flesh of Jesus but also through the imagination of God. As we read, we are pushed to imagine just how far-reaching the love of God expands. This expansion is, no doubt, the main issue for the religious elite in Jesus's context.

In today's polarizing climate, wars and debates rage online that all too often dehumanize our own brothers and sisters in Christ. Shane Claiborne puts it best when he says: "The seeds of the gospel are really small. They're really about meeting God at dinner tables and in living rooms and in the little towns that may not be known to the rest of the world. But it seems like that's exactly what happens when God moves into the neighborhood in Jesus . . . it's that which I think we're invited into is to grow into a neighborhood, to plant ourselves somewhere and to get to know people there, and to see seeds of the kingdom grown there."

King Jesus, in moving into the neighborhood (John 1:14), moved into the messiness and complexities of his neighbors. At times it appeared chaotic, impulsive, and emotional to religious onlookers. But Jesus's only driving force was pure love—the kind of love that may have appeared to be chaotic and impulsive, but it was a holy chaos and a holy impulse. In the chaos and the mess, Jesus saw the broken and hurting for who they were and met them in their pain and bruises. He saw the prostitutes, tax collectors, and notorious sinners as image bearers. And what Jesus offered was a path to liberation and holiness—not shame, guilt, or judgment.

Today, it seems Christians are more known for what they stand against rather than whom they stand for. Dear ones, I don't know about you, but I thank King Jesus for pursuing me, seeing me, finding me, loving me, and showing me the path to liberation and holiness—and never through shame, guilt, or judgment. Jesus, in his relentless love, has given me a family to call my own, a hope for the future, an aching for the mission, and freedom from sin. I yearn to participate in this same mission that Jesus is on—pursuing those in desperate need of the life-changing message of Christ.

As followers of Jesus, may we allow God's story to form our imaginations of whom we should pursue and whom we should engage. Jesus was in the wild; the messy, chaotic, and broken wild. Brothers and sisters in Christ, more than ever, it's time.

It's time to, in the power of the Spirit, discover the wild for the glory of God's kingdom.

Pray

Living Lord, forgive me for the ways I do not love my neighbor as I love myself. Forgive me for the ways I look down on those who aren't like me and the ways I harbor bitterness in my heart. Lord, forgive me for the biases I sometimes allow to manifest in my heart and then in my actions. God, break my heart for what breaks yours. Give me eyes to see my neighborhood as you see it. Give me a heart for my community as you have. Give me a fresh imagination, birthed from your Spirit and drenched in your love. Lord, empower me to be your hands and feet to all whom I encounter today. Amen.

APRIL 1, 2019

written by Tara Beth Leach

Read

Revelation 19:1–8

Additional: Leviticus 23:26–41 • Psalm 53

Reflect

In the beginning, there was power. Pure, unhindered, creative power. God spoke, and light permeated the universe. God spoke, and the seas thundered, and the mountains trembled. God spoke and, in God's creative power, painted the grand tapestry on which we now stand. God spoke, gathered dirt, and breathed life into the lungs of bodies. These bodies were given names, personalities, imaginations, and the gift of power. Yes, power. These bodies with names, personalities, and imaginations were given the gift of stewarding God's power—rooted in the love of God for the good of God's creation.

But we have not stewarded the incredible gift of power well. Since the outset of God's story, the temptation to usurp the authority of God has been at the forefront. We have used power for our own personal gain. We have used it to coerce, destroy, oppress, and harm. We became so intoxicated with this idea of being rulers that we attempted to be God. We have built empires, kingdoms, Babylons, and societies birthed from the coercive and oppressive powers of this present world. The reality of Babylon is everywhere. Yet the story is headed somewhere.

In Christ, a new kind of kingdom is ushered in—one where the world's power structures are obliterated at last. Power is life-giving, creative, liberating, and restorative. Soon and very soon, Babylon will be ushered out as the great symphony of God's people will roar, "Hallelujah! For our Lord God Almighty reigns. Let us rejoice and be glad and give him glory!"

The bride of the Lamb—that is, the people of God—will someday experience the fullness of her groom, the risen and ascended Lord, King Jesus, as the shadowy, evil powers are disarmed at last. Even so, God's redeeming power is presently shaping, forming, and transforming the surrendered people of God into Christlikeness. In the middle of a chaotic and broken world, the call of the bride is to submit herself to the Lamb's agenda. In other words, we don't take our cues from worldly powers; rather, we take our cues from the Lamb who was laid down for all.

Pray

Lord Jesus, may we never forget who is the King. May everything we do on this earth point to your glory and to the glory of our Father in heaven. Amen.

APRIL 2, 2019

written by Tara Beth Leach

Read

Revelation 19:9–10

Additional: Leviticus 25:1–19 • Psalm 53

Reflect

The image of the worshiping community in the book of Revelation is awe-inspiring. The worship we practice during our weekly gatherings is a foretaste of the future kingdom of God, no doubt. But, more than likely, you've heard one of these statements, or something like it:
"I'm just not feeling the worship today."
"I don't need to worship at a church; I can just do it at home with online sermons and my worship playlist."
"I'm not being fed on Sunday mornings."
"I can't worship to that style of music."

You get the drift. It's often a kick in the gut for pastors to hear something like this, although not on a personal level so much as for how it reveals a lack of theological imagination for the very purpose of our gathering. Statements like these are not birthed from a biblical understanding of worship; rather, they come from a marketplace-culture understanding of worship. An understanding of worship that is: About me. For me. About my needs being met. About my preferences.

It is critical that we push back against the false notion that has emerged in the Western church about the purpose of our gathering and what it is for. There is a notion that this gathering is only about a very personal encounter with God and nothing else; that the purpose of the gathering is about me; that the purpose of the gathering is for my comfort only. We have somehow wrongly allowed the Western marketplace culture to seep into our spaces of worship. When we limit the purpose of worship to a personal encounter with God, preference wars can become prevalent. You've heard it:

"I encounter God only when we sing (insert band name) songs."
"I can only encounter God with the pipe organ and the hymnal!"

People leave churches and find new ones because of preference wars. This attitude sounds much more distinctly Consumer than Christian. While we are, no doubt, personally and individually strengthened in worship, and while we do encounter a very personal God, when we limit our worship expectations, we are only limiting our imaginations about what it means to be distinctly sent (see Acts 1:8).

The weekly gathering, which includes worship through song, prayer, Eucharist, fellowship, and the proclamation of the written Word, is a distinguishing activity for Christians all around the world. And in this unique way of singing, eating, preaching, praying, and fellowshipping, we are formed as a people. Not only that, but when we gather, we are the holy temple of God. We—the people of God, the Christian congregation—are God's dwelling place. When we gather together as God's holy temple, we are recalling the promises of God and responding in worship, adoration, and praise for God's unending faithfulness and presence. As we gather in God's presence, we are being formed, shaped, and transformed into God's likeness. As Paul so pastorally reminds us, "And we all, who with unveiled faces contemplate the Lord's glory, are being transformed into his image with ever-increasing glory, which comes from the Lord, who is the Spirit" (2 Cor. 3:18). As we are formed into his likeness, we step into our neighborhoods with a unique love, grace, and joy, and the Christian engages the world in the posture of Jesus, who lays down his life for his friends, neighbors, and strangers.

As we respond to the presence and action of God, we use our unique gifts to edify and encourage one another to live out in everyday life the holy mission that is given to us through the faithfulness of God, the crucified, risen, and ascended King Jesus, and the empowering presence of the Spirit. The people of God actively respond to a God who acts first, moves in, and engages God's people while forming them in God's likeness and shaping them for mission.

As Christians, we should be desperate to come back together every week. We live in a challenging world that can make us weary. As the Christian people of God, we have a unique, countercultural, and distinct way of singing, eating, talking, proclaiming, and praying. What we do in gathering together has disciple-making, transformative power—that is, what we do in the gathering has *sending* power.

Pray

Lord, I pray that you would reform my perspective in the weekly worship gathering. Forgive me for the ways that I seek to consume only, instead of using my gifts to edify my brothers and sisters. Lord, I pray that your Spirit would propel me from the sidelines and into the game. I pray that I would have a renewed passion for the weekly worship gathering, and I pray that you would begin preparing my heart today for the gathering. Amen.

written by Tara Beth Leach

Read

Luke 9:10–17

Additional: 2 Kings 4:1–7 • Psalm 53

Reflect

"You can't be serious!" I said out loud as the students shouted my name.

"Pastor Tara Beth, Pastor Tara Beth, jump! Jump!"

I was a new youth pastor, eager to impress my students, but this just seemed like too big of a leap. I stood on a two-foot-tall tower, holding onto a rope swing that would soon carry me into a lake. A family in our church had the tradition of throwing a lake party for students, and the highlight was the rope swing. But when I climbed the tower and looked at the lake and considered my own upper-body strength, I just didn't know if I could make the leap. But the students continued to chant, and finally, after some taunts and teasing, I jumped.

The story of Jesus feeding the crowd with just five loaves of bread and only two fish is a story of trust. The disciples were concerned that the crowd was hungry, and they attempted to solve the problem in the most obvious way—sending the people away from Jesus and into the surrounding villages to buy food for themselves.

But Jesus pushed the envelope. "You feed them."

I imagine some eye-rolls from the disciples, and even some mockery in their thoughts and hearts: *Jesus must be out of his mind.* But he wasn't; he just had a divine imagination. The disciples' imaginations were limited, but Jesus's was God-sized.

Then the disciples had a choice. Would they trust and obey Jesus? I imagine they were rather tempted to usurp Jesus's authority in this situation and take matters into their own hands. Remarkably, however, the disciples took one faithful step after the next, showing us the radical posture that trust requires.

We live in a world that has an explanation and solutions for virtually everything. But some things can't always be explained. Some things are God-sized, audacious, beyond our human strategies.

I've often heard a pastor or two say that if our dreams can be accomplished by our own effort, then perhaps our dreams aren't God's dreams. Perhaps our imaginations are driven by our own agendas, strategies, and aspirations. Not only that, but when God calls, it sometimes requires a blind leap of faith by simply putting one foot in front of the other.

God-sized dreams demand radical trust and obedience, but they also require that we begin in a posture of prayer and surrender. God-sized dreams can't be conjured up on a white board; rather, God's imagination is birthed from the very heart of God through God's people. It's tempting to get ahead of God and take matters into our own hands, but perhaps today you begin by simply asking what God's dreams are for your life. Begin by getting to know the heart of God through reading Scripture and through prayer. Take time to listen to God. Over time, God's heart will be revealed, and those God-sized dreams will become clear. Then we will discover the adventurous life that requires bold leaps of faith in the power of the Spirit.

Pray

Living Lord, thank you for the gift of today. I confess that there are days when I choose my own path instead of yours. I confess that sometimes my dreams are birthed out of my own ambitions rather than yours. I confess that my dreams have been shaped by the world rather than the Word. Today, Lord, I pray that your Spirit would begin to chisel away at my selfish ambitions and replace them with yours. Open my imagination for a life drenched in your Spirit, empowered to step into new horizons. Help me put to death the things that are not of you, and birth within me something so big that it drives me to my knees. Help me to see the world as you see it, and help me to see my gifts, my mind, my hands, and my feet as you see them—vessels and tools for your glory. Lord, I long to bring you honor and glory in all things. I pray that your Spirit would guide me step by step, breath by breath, and moment by moment. I trust you today, Lord. Amen.

APRIL 4, 2019

written by Tara Beth Leach

Read

Philippians 2:19–24

Additional: Psalm 126 • Isaiah 43:1–7

Reflect

When we dig into the vision of discipleship that is rooted in Scripture, we discover that it has less to do with head knowledge and more to do with life lived. Of course, our theology is lived, and sound doctrine and theology are critical—but not at the cost of living counter to the cruciform life (that is, imitating the way of Jesus).

The apostle Paul, in describing his brother and partner in the gospel, Timothy, highlights Timothy's genuine concern for others. In contrast, Paul notes the tendency most people have to look out only for their own interests and not those of Jesus Christ. Not much has changed a couple thousand years later. In today's world, we celebrate passion, talent, intellect, power, and achievement while day-to-day acts of kindness go unnoticed. Yet, without genuine love of neighbor, the Christian life is a counterfeit version of Jesus's vision for the kingdom.

Love of God and neighbor are central to the kingdom vision Jesus proclaimed when he walked the dusty roads of this earth. Jesus then showed it to us as a way of life as he journeyed to the cross. This is the cruciform life, yet our tendency is to put ourselves first. "Me first" may very well be at the root of division in the church.

"My needs aren't being met."
"I'm not feeling the pastor's preaching."
"I don't like the music."
"I'm right, and you're wrong."

But the heart and teachings of Jesus sound more like:

"You first."
"I'll serve you."
"How can I meet your needs?"
"I forgive you."

The bride of Christ should live in a way—the cruciform way— that is stunningly different in contrast to the way of the world. But sometimes it seems that the bride of Christ's ways are blurred with the world's ways.

As a holy people and a royal priesthood, we have been chosen and empowered to express the heart of God in this world. In doing so we are participating in the redemption of all creation and in God's mission. As sons and daughters of the King and as imitators of Christ, we should evoke curiosity in the eyes of the world.

The season of Lent is the perfect time for recalibration, centering, and examination. Consider taking an inventory of your attitudes, actions, and postures toward others. Consider prayerfully journaling and examining the following:
- The words you say and the way you speak them
- Your vocational choices
- Your financial practices

- Your recreational pursuits and hobbies
- Your actions toward others

Furthermore, consider the things that have been shaping and forming your attitude. Consider prayerfully journaling and examining the following:
- The people who surround you
- The television shows you watch
- The magazines you read
- The daily habits you have

Consider how these practices form you to be oriented either toward a me-first attitude or a someone-else-first attitude. Are these practices forming you to be more like Christ or less like Christ? As you prayerfully take an inventory of your life, know that it is not met with condemnation; rather, it is met with the grace and love of God. God's grace frees us from our selfish attitudes and empowers us. But it begins on our knees with a posture of surrender. God desires a willing and obedient heart.

Pray

Living Lord, I humble myself before you. As I look into the mirror of my soul and character, expose the very things that are postured toward myself rather than others. God, I thank you that your grace meets me exactly as I am, but I pray that I won't stay here. I pray that the Spirit of the living God would shape and form me to live a life oriented toward you and others. Help me to love you with everything and also to love my neighbor relentlessly, as you do. Help me change any practices in my life that are forming me away from your likeness, and help me discover new practices that propel me toward your transforming grace. I need you, Lord. Amen.

APRIL 5, 2019

written by Tara Beth Leach

Read

Philippians 2:25–3:1

Additional: Psalm 126 • Isaiah 43:8–15

Reflect

Paul is an apostle, a pastor, a missionary, and an evangelist. As a pastor, Paul writes his letters from the depths of his heart to the people for whom he cares so tenderly. He cares about his coworkers who join him in the mission of God. In this passage, Paul is particularly concerned about his brother, co-worker, and fellow soldier who is also a messenger to the church in Philippi. Paul sends comforting words so they will know that he is well after a near-death experience, and Paul admonishes the church to care for Epaphroditus.

This passage is a good reminder for Christians to remember to care for pastors, missionaries, evangelists, and servants of the Lord. In today's consumer culture, churches can demand a lot from pastors, and pastors all too often burn out. Though it is truly life-giving for a pastor to serve her or his congregation, congregations often forget to care for their pastors. There might be seasons in your pastor's life when they need extra time to rest, or better boundaries, or extra care. Remember that your pastor is human and needs to be edified and encouraged just like you.

All pastors have folks in their congregation who have the gift of discouragement, and then there are those who have the gift of encouragement. Which are you?

As a pastor myself, Mondays tend to be particularly hard days for me. These tend to be the days when frustrated congregants write emails about all the things that dissatisfied them on Sunday. It isn't uncommon for me to wake up to an email or two from someone who has been harboring frustration or bitterness for the last twenty-four hours. Monday is also the day when I am most likely to be feeling depleted and vulnerable. Finally, if Sunday's offering was particularly low, Monday is when I find out.

Not too long ago, word got out that I wasn't a fan of Mondays. One congregant wrote me an email one Monday morning to begin to counteract that trend. Then another group got together and wrote me a card of encouragement every Monday for several months. I then made it a practice to read the encouraging cards before opening my emails that day. The cards always contained the right words for me at the right time. The Holy Spirit often highlighted the words I needed for that day. Small gestures go a long way toward making your church leader a better pastor.

Consider how you might embody the gift of encouragement for your pastor today. Here are a few ideas:
- Pray for your pastor.
- Write a card.
- Go out of your way every now and then to tell your pastor something you appreciate about them.
- Ask your pastor how you can specifically support her or him.
- Send your pastor (and their spouse, if applicable) out to dinner.
- If your pastor has children, let them know how appreciated they are.

- If you ever overhear someone speaking gossip, slander, or negativity about your pastor, stop the conversation.

Pray

Living Lord, I thank you for my pastor today. Help me to be an encourager instead of a discourager. Help me to care better for my pastor and protect the office of the pastor. Give me wisdom and discernment on how to be a support. I pray for my pastor today. When she or he is weary, may you give her or him strength. When my pastor is discouraged, I pray that you would highlight words that would encourage her or him. I pray that our pastor would find ties of rest and nourishment so that she or he can live in your strength instead of their own. I pray that we as a church would edify our pastor just as much as she or he edifies us. Forgive me that I often make church about me. I know it's all about you and your vision. Help our church live into the vision of a holy community: edifying, encouraging, loving, and comforting. Amen.

SATURDAY
APRIL 6, 2019

written by Tara Beth Leach

Read

John 11:45–57

Additional: Exodus 12:21-27 • Psalm 126

Reflect

The climax of Jesus's ministry was winding down, and the cross was now imminent. As threats against Jesus's life increased, Jesus withdrew to the wilderness.

My husband, Jeff, and I live in a little mountain town in southern California, just outside Los Angeles, and we love the wilderness. We spend a lot of time exploring and hiking. Not too long ago, we decided to do an overnight backpacking trip in the mountains. We spent months preparing and researching how to survive in the wilderness. When the day came, we mounted our heavy packs with all the supplies we could possibly need—except whatever we'd need to defend ourselves from a bear.

After hiking all day, we were finally ready to set up camp. We pulled out of our bags everything we needed to sustain us for the next few days, including food, clothing, and a water-filtration system. We were ready to survive the wilderness! To our shock, however, we were visited by a very hungry bear that was not fazed in any way by our attempts to scare it away. We finally decided it would be safer for us to get out of there. Once we reached the safety of our car and left the campsite, we breathed a sigh of relief. We were so happy to be out of the wilderness.

Wilderness is a powerful theme throughout the story of God. The wilderness represents scarcity, loneliness, vulnerability, and longing. The wilderness is often a place of the already-but-not-yet, or a place between chapters. The wilderness is a place between two somewheres, longing to get from one somewhere to the other somewhere. Jesus and the Israelites knew the wilderness well, and perhaps you do too.

Perhaps you have been waiting for a significant relationship, or have ended one. Perhaps you've been looking for a particular job, or one was ripped out from underneath you. Perhaps you've been wandering and searching for a purpose but wonder if you even have one. Or maybe you've stepped into unfamiliar territory and are longing for a sense of home. So here you are, full of questions, doubts, aches, fears, and longing for what could be. As difficult as the wilderness might be, Scripture reminds us time and time again that there are powerful lessons to be learned there. In the wilderness, we learn the true posture of dependence on the Lord. We might feel naked and vulnerable, but we are invited to discover the Bread of Life and the living Water.

The temptation in the wilderness is to resort to negativity, complaining, and bitterness. Consider the Israelites. After God rescued them from the oppressive grip of Pharaoh and miraculously parted the Red Sea, the Israelites found themselves in a place of discomfort, vulnerability, and wandering. It didn't take long for them to resort to negative groaning. This is the tendency that we as humans have when we are in a less than ideal situation. Not only that, but we might be tempted to survive the wilderness by our own self-sufficiency. Let us not miss out on the powerful lessons of the wilderness. Without the vulnerability, brokenness, and dryness of the wilderness, we may never fully discover that God, our daily bread, is all we need. When we learn to depend on God, and when we ditch the never-ending drive to accomplish, we might discover the adventurous life that is found in Christ.

Pray

Living Lord, the wilderness is hard. I feel lonely, vulnerable, lost, scared, and confused. I confess that I too often posture myself like a know-it-all before you. I confess that I have attempted to carve my way through the wilderness in my own strength and with my own ideas. I don't want to miss out on the lessons of the wilderness. Give me patience, wisdom, and nourishment. Help me discover the depths of trust and dependence. Do something in my life that only you can do during this season. Give me a vision of hope in the God who is with us, who will put the world right, and who is presently reordering the world and infusing peace. Amen.

FIFTH SUNDAY IN LENT

April 7, 2019

written by Tara Beth Leach

Read

John 12:1–8

Additional: Psalm 126 • Isaiah 43:16–21 • Philippians 3:4b–14

Reflect

Jesus travels through Bethany on his way to Jerusalem. He has just performed perhaps one of the most significant miracles in his journey. Many are awe-inspired, curious, and want to discover Jesus, the prophet who raises people from the dead. Mary, a devoted follower of Jesus, is especially awe-inspired since the person Jesus raised from the dead is her brother. Mary shows extravagant gratitude by kneeling at the feet of Jesus and anointing his feet with pure nard. The nard signifies her recognition that Jesus isn't just anyone; rather, she is proclaiming Jesus as King. As she lets her hair down, she shows humility and devotion to Jesus, but others at the dinner party are appalled by her seeming waste.

Throughout the Gospels, we consistently see Mary's posture of extreme devotion to Jesus. When Jesus came to visit her and her sister, Martha, Mary made herself totally available to Jesus and his teachings. As she sat at his feet, wrapped up in his teachings, locked in on every word, focused in the moment, her sister, Martha, was "worried about many things" (Luke 10:41). In contrast, time and time again, we are able to observe Mary wrapped up in, locked in on, totally focused on, completely available to, and wholly devoted to her master.

When I was sixteen, my dad handed me the keys to his beloved Hummer to drive to school. I was so excited that I picked up a group of girlfriends, and off we went. We were chatting, listening to music, hollering out the windows, and having a good ol' time when, suddenly, we heard a BAM and SCREEEECH. I had been so consumed by the excitement of the moment that I had stopped paying attention to where I was driving and drove off the road, into a giant metal pedestrian sign. The side of my dad's Hummer looked as though someone had taken a knife from the front of the vehicle all the way to the brake lights. I knew I was doomed.

We live in a world full of distractions that seek to pull us away from extreme devotion to and love for Jesus. Opportunities surround us daily that seek to lead us off course. Places to go, things to see, more to accomplish, shiny-big things to buy, and careers to pursue. While not all distraction is bad, it can quickly turn into idolatry if we let it, and before we know it, our Christian journey can veer off course toward the path of destruction.

Consider what your daily life would look like with the same posture of devotion that Mary exhibits. How would you order your day? How would you spend the first hour of your morning? What would you say to the living Lord before you close your eyes to sleep? What kinds of things would fill your mind? How would you spend your Sundays or Fridays? The call to discipleship is a call to a life that is wrapped up in, locked in on, totally focused on, completely available to, and wholly devoted to our Master.

Ultimately, Mary's posture of devotion is birthed out of love and gratitude for the goodness Jesus displayed through the miracle of Lazarus, her brother. When we consider the life, the teachings, the fulfillment, the death, the resurrection, and the ascension of King Jesus, who has given us the gift of life, belonging, and freedom, how could we not order our day in a way that shows extreme gratitude?

Pray

Living Lord, I thank you for the grace and goodness you have lavished upon your people. I know I do not deserve the gift you have given me, and I thank you that you've poured it out anyway. Forgive me for the ways I, time and time again, fail to express my gratitude. Forgive me for the ways some of the world's distractions quickly turn into a path to destruction and idolatry. Lord, today I choose to express my devotion, love, and need for you. Today I choose to be wrapped up in, locked in on, totally focused on, completely available to, and wholly devoted to you. I love you, Lord; I need you, Lord. Amen.

APRIL 8, 2019

written by Tara Beth Leach

Read

Hebrews 10:19–25

Additional: Exodus 40:1–15 • Psalm 20

Reflect

It's easy to notice not everyone attends church on Sunday mornings. I see them out running, having coffee in their sweatpants, biking, mowing lawns. As we can see from the letter to the Hebrews, faithfully gathering to worship together on a regular basis isn't a new practice. We see it even earlier than Hebrews, in fact, as the earliest model for worship in the Christian church (see Acts 2:42). Faithfully gathering together has been central since the birth of the church. But I can offer plenty of good reasons *not* to gather.

1. Don't attend church if you're looking for a club where everyone talks alike, looks alike, and dresses alike. Don't come to church if you're looking for a dominant culture or socioeconomic status. Don't come to church if you're looking for an exclusive organization that rejects anyone who doesn't fit a certain profile. When you come to church, look into the eyes

of someone who isn't like you, who doesn't look like you, and who comes from a different walk of life.

2. Don't attend church if you're looking for easy answers. Life happens. Life is complex. We wrestle with theology. Not a single Christian has all the answers. Instead, when you come to church, be open to new things. Be open to being challenged. Be open to new ideas. Come with an open heart and mind, and know that you may not walk away with all of life's answers figured out.

3. Don't attend church if you're looking for a place to always and only be filled up and never poured out. If you're coming to only consume, you're going to be disappointed. Don't attend church if you're looking for entertainment. When you gather together, you might get a pastor who minces words now and then, or who sometimes preaches a sermon that doesn't move you like it did the week before. You might see music leaders who may not always hit the exact note. Some Sundays the music might be too loud, too quiet, you might sing too many hymns, or you may not sing enough hymns. Instead, come to church to bless someone else. Come to use your gifts of teaching, preaching, leading, encouraging, praying, admonishing, caring, and edifying. Come to bless, and while you're at it, you will be blessed.

4. Don't attend church if you don't want to be stretched and pushed. Don't attend the worship gathering if you want to stay comfortable. When you come, you're going to hear things you don't like. Don't come if you're hoping you're going to agree with every single thing, or if you're looking to maintain status quo. If you don't want to be stretched or pushed, don't come. The demands of discipleship are costly, and Christians tend to hold one another accountable. The Holy Spirit convicts us and makes us uncomfortable. Pastors preach about living the mission of God. The pushing, convicting, and piercing words of Jesus are often read out loud. Don't come to church if you don't want to be stretched or pushed.

The gospel—that is, the life, fulfillment, teachings, death, resurrection, and ascension of King Jesus—wasn't given so you could be propelled into an exceptionally individual life. Instead, the gospel propels us into life together, as a holy people. And when we gather together, we share that common commitment and confession: God is love; Jesus is alive; Jesus is King; the Spirit of God has been poured out for all! When we gather, we are making a countercultural declaration of the countercultural values of the kingdom of God: Jesus is Lord, and Caesar is not. We are declaring that, in a world of death, decay, destruction, pain, and violence, the shalom of God is bursting forth. When we gather, we are declaring and professing the God who makes all things new.

We need a place where we can reorient our minds and be reminded of what actually matters. We need a place where others hold us accountable to living into the purposes of God. Without church, I am absolutely convinced that we cannot stay faithful to the purposes of God. As I always say to my precious congregation in Southern California, "I need you; you need me; we need you; you need us."

Pray

Lord, you are my daily bread, the air that I breathe, and the living water. You are what I need more than anything, and I also know that I can't do this without your people. I thank you for the gift of the worship gathering, and I don't want to take it for granted. I pray that I would make the most of the worship gathering, and I pray that you would renew my love and passion for faithful worship. Amen.

APRIL 9, 2019

written by Tara Beth Leach

Read

1 John 2:18–28

Additional: Judges 9:7–15 • Psalm 20

Reflect

Echoes of Jesus's words from John can be heard in this passage from 1 John: "I am the vine; you are the branches. If you remain in me and I in you, you will bear much fruit; apart from me you can do nothing. If you do not remain in me, you are like a branch that is thrown away and withers; such branches are picked up, thrown into the fire and burned. If you remain in me and my words remain in you, ask whatever you wish, and it will be done for you. This is to my Father's glory, that you bear much fruit, showing yourselves to be my disciples" (John 15:5–8).

John's letter to the early church recalls some of the same teachings of Jesus. Remain in Jesus. John so pastorally writes his letter in hopes that his words will encourage the early church not to drift away.

Drifting away from our relationship with Jesus is often so gradual that it can happen without us even realizing it. Recently, I walked through a very crowded airport with both of my boys. They were excited that we were soon boarding a plane to go see Nana and Papa, and I was hurrying them along so we wouldn't miss our flight. Since my arms were full of bags, I instructed the boys to hang on to me so we wouldn't get separated. We've nicknamed our youngest son, Noah, "Wonder Boy." The smallest things can grab his attention and distract him from the task at hand. As we scurried along, I turned around to discover that Noah was suddenly nowhere to be found. I pushed my way through the crowds, calling out his name as panic began to set in.

Five minutes later—an agonizingly long time for a six-year-old to be lost in a big airport—a security guard came walking down the hallway with Noah. Noah's big brown eyes immediately welled up with giant elephant tears. I pulled him close and asked, "Noah, what happened! Where did you go?!"

"I don't know," Noah cried. He didn't know how it happened, but I could easily imagine that something had caught his eye and, before he knew it, caused him to drift away from the family.

Jesus lovingly invites his followers to remain in him because, when we do, we will bear fruit that reflects the image, heart, and character of God. But many of us have such crowded, busy, and overwhelmed lives that it doesn't take long before we are lost in the sea of distractions. As these distractions begin to hijack our own hearts, we eventually drift away from our relationship with Jesus without even realizing.

Have we, then, settled for a shallow relationship with Jesus? Like a young plant that needs supports to keep it from withering, we too need intentional structure and support. Without intentional structure, we risk limping along haphazardly in a tangled-up, disordered, and diminished walk with Jesus. Regular structure— morning and evening prayers, Bible reading, solitude, retreats, Sunday worship, and accountability—gives us the freedom to grow as we were meant to. Patterns of discipline help us grow into the image of Jesus.

Pray

Living Lord, you are so good to me. Thank you for your grace that meets me where I am. Thank you for your grace that seeks me out in the crowd, in the midst of the many distractions. I know I am prone to drift. Give me wisdom on how to intentionally order my life so I can remember that you are my source. You are my sustainer. You are my Bread of Life. You are my living water. Forgive me that I live as though my own strength is enough. Today I choose to turn from the things pulling me away from you. Today I choose to intentionally order my life around the rhythms of your grace. Help me practice your presence moment by moment, minute by minute, second by second, and breath by breath. I long to be transformed by your grace in such a way that the world sees you and your goodness in me. Amen.

WEDNESDAY
APRIL 10, 2019

written by Tara Beth Leach

Read

Luke 18:31–34

Additional: Psalm 20 • Habakkuk 3:2–15

Reflect

As a pastor, a question I hear a lot is, "How do I get to heaven?" Christians have argued the answer to this question down through the decades, and it is, no doubt, important to wrestle with, but I think we could get better at asking questions. Of course, none of us would prefer any assumed alternative to heaven. Still, though, perhaps we might ask instead, *If Jesus is King, how should I live?*

In this particular passage in Luke, the disciples find the words of Jesus to be rather peculiar. Up until this point, things have been going pretty well. Jesus has performed many signs, wonders, and miracles; the disciples are starting to grasp his teachings; Jesus has a decent following. But now, Jesus's words might as well be a record scratch. The disciples likely wonder whether Jesus is sleep deprived, stressed, overwhelmed, hallucinating. Jesus is pushing the envelope far beyond what the disciples can comprehend. This teaching, however, begins to expand the imagination of the very nature and character of Jesus. Through this proclamation, we see the lengths to which Jesus goes as the Son of God; through this proclamation, we discover that Jesus came to serve, not to be served.

If Jesus is King, how should I live?

If Jesus is King, then the people in the kingdom live as the King lives. The people of the kingdom are oriented toward the things the King is oriented toward. We lay down our lives just as the King laid down his life. In a world that says me first, the King says *you first.* The people in the kingdom love those whom the King loves. The people in the kingdom pursue those whom the King pursues. We pursue the lost, the broken, and the hurting. We love them and lift them up as the King lifts them up. We show them the hospitality and love of Jesus.

As a mother of two, one of my greatest joys is watching my two precious boys mimic their father. My husband, Jeff, is quite the Mr. Fix-it and is often seen with a tool in his hand, whether in the house or underneath a car. My oldest son, Caleb, often follows his daddy around the house with a toy hammer or screwdriver, mimicking Jeff. Not too long ago, Jeff was working underneath a car, so Caleb ran inside to grab his toolbox and began "fixing" his fire truck. Jeff played along, propping up the fire truck so Caleb could get underneath.

Caleb follows in the footsteps of his daddy so much that he is becoming just like him. As his mother, I watch his mannerisms, his phrases, and his actions and think, *Wow, that is just like Jeff.* Living like the King means we mimic him. We mimic his actions. We mimic his phrases. We look and act so much like him that we remind people of him when they see us.

Where are your eyes? Today, choose to fix them on the King.

Pray

Lord, you amaze me. The fact that you came to serve is at times beyond comprehension. Much like the disciples were bewildered by your teachings of the cross, I find myself bewildered at times too. I pray that you would stretch my imagination for the life you are calling me to live. Give me a vision for the kingdom life—a life that looks a lot like you. I pray that your Spirit would transform my heart and mind in such a way that my thoughts and actions reflect your nature and character. You are my strength today. I love you. Amen.

Read

Hebrews 2:1–9

Additional: Psalm 31:9–16 • Isaiah 53:10–12

Reflect

Imagine being in the disciples' shoes in the last year of Jesus's ministry. Their feet are blistered and weary. They have labored almost three long years, and they left everything, including their family, friends, vacations, and comfort. But it has been seemingly worth it. They've witnessed signs, wonders, and miracles. Before their very eyes, Jesus has healed the lame, raised the dead, fed thousands with a measly amount of food, healed the blind, and loved the outcast. They've heard Jesus teach a vision of a new kind of kingdom: one of love, hospitality, generosity, diversity, and unity. It is radically different than anything they've ever heard.

But then: "We are going up to Jerusalem, and the Son of Man will be delivered over to the chief priests and the teachers of the law. They will condemn him to death and will hand him over to the Gentiles to be mocked and flogged and crucified. On the third day he will be raised to life!" (Matthew 20:18–19). Wait, what? The disciples must be worried by this statement; things have been going so well. Why is Jesus talking about suffering?

It doesn't take long before the haunting words of Jesus begin to play out before the disciples' very eyes, and eventually Jesus is crucified. Now the same disciples who were once hopeful are full of despair, guilt, confusion, and sorrow.

We know the gloriousness of Easter, which we will soon celebrate. We know that sin, despair, guilt, confusion, sorrow, and darkness did not get the last word. The disciples saw the dawn of Easter with their own eyes and laid down their futures to participate in proclaiming this gift to the nations.

The gift of salvation dispels the powers of darkness, sin, shame, brokenness, and evil. How, as the writer of Hebrews so beautifully declares, can we ignore this? The disciples were never the same. How about you? Have you allowed the gift of salvation to get the last word over your life? Have you allowed the transforming light to turn your heart away from sin, shame, and brokenness?

Consider the lengths Jesus went to for us. Remember today the incredible gift that dispels the power of darkness. Reflect on the good news of the gospel. Give thanks to God.

Pray

Living Lord, when I reflect on the faithfulness of King Jesus, I am in awe of the grandeur of your beauty and love. I confess there are days that I act as though I don't appreciate this gift. I confess there are days when I choose gifts that the world has to offer over yours. I confess that I am ungrateful, callous, and lukewarm. Restore unto me the joy of my salvation. Renew within me a heart of gratitude. Renew within me a desire to live in such a way that reflects your illuminating image. I love you, Lord. Amen.

APRIL 12, 2019

written by Tara Beth Leach

Read

Isaiah 54:9–10

Additional: Psalm 31:9–16 • Hebrews 2:10–18

Reflect

Have you ever spent time with someone who struggles to follow through with their commitments? Or someone who talks extravagantly but whose life doesn't match their words? Or have you ever known someone who *is* faithful to always follow through on their commitments and who always does what they say they will do?

In Scripture, the very nature and character of God is revealed, and situated in the heart of God is faithfulness. God's promises are true. God is who he says he is, and God will do what he says he will do.

In the beginning, we discover a God who is serious about putting the world right. While it doesn't take long for God's people to go awry, God actively moves in with grace, love, tenderness, and compassion. And, through the covenants, we discover God's plan of redemption. And as that plan unfolds, God's people time and time again abandon their commitments to God. The people of God are untrustworthy, unreliable, and fickle. It's a wonder God doesn't give up.

Instead, through the covenant community's disobedience, God's faithfulness is all the more revealed and magnified. God's steadfast love is poured out through the faithfulness of King Jesus, and as the faithfulness of God reaches its pinnacle, we discover just how serious God is about restoration. In our unfaithfulness, God is faithful. In our callousness, God is loving. In our stubbornness, God relentlessly pursues. In our sinfulness, God is gracious. In our hard-headedness, God is beautifully brilliant.

Dear ones, let these words settle into your heart for a moment: God is faithful. God will not abandon you. God is your daily bread. God will set the world right. God hears you. God includes you in God's plan. God faithfully loves you. God is our provider. God meets you where you are. God is faithful.

Do you trust in God's faithfulness? And as you learn to trust in God's faithfulness, can God trust in yours? As we learn to trust in God's faithfulness, we must also discover the invitation to participate in covenant faithfulness. Can God trust you to steward God's gifts well? Can God trust you to care for God's people well? Can God trust you to use your power graciously, creatively, and generously? Can God trust that you will obey God's commands?

Consider areas of your life in which you have been faithful, and consider the areas in which you have been unfaithful.

Pray

Lord, great is your faithfulness. When I think about your goodness that is magnified in your covenants and in the faithfulness of King Jesus, I tremble. I tremble at your faithfulness to me, even when I'm not faith-

ful in return. I'm grateful for your grace that meets me even in these moments. God, you are so good to me. It's difficult for me to comprehend where I would be if not for you. I pray that you would form my heart into a trustworthy heart. I pray that I would not only learn to trust and believe in your faithfulness, but I pray that I would also be faithful. Amen.

APRIL 13, 2019

written by Tara Beth Leach

Read

Luke 22:1–13

Additional: Leviticus 23:1–8 • Psalm 31:9–16

Reflect

Several months ago, a friend sent me away to a hotel in San Francisco so I could meet a major writing deadline. While I was there, I somehow locked myself in the hotel bathroom. Thankfully, I had my cell phone with me, but that didn't keep me from mortification at the entire experience. When the hotel crew came to rescue me from the bathroom, one employee exclaimed, "This happens all the time!"

Confused, I said, "Do you think that perhaps the doors are the problem, then?"

I often wonder if we are like this in our Christian lives—if we sometimes function with sin and darkness in our hearts without ever acknowledging it until it manifests in ugly ways. We all have dark, broken, and sinful secrets locked away in our hearts. We bury them deep in an attempt to cover them up. "Nothing to see here! I'm good!"

In the days leading up to the cross, Judas had secrets tucked away in his heart. Although he looked like he was loyal to Jesus, something else was brewing. So it was with Cain and Abel. Sin crept in at Cain's door, and eventually leading to the Bible's first recorded murder.

What are the secrets of your heart? During this season of Lent, pray for the light to shine into the darkness in your heart and expose your secrets. But as they are exposed, trust that there is no shame in the light. Instead, know that God is still for you and that your secrets aren't met with condemnation; rather, they are met with transforming grace.

God is for you, even with the dark secrets of the heart. God is for you, even in what you haven't accomplished. God is for you, even with your failures. God is for you, even with your anger. God is for you, even with your past mistakes. God is for you, even with your sin and brokenness. God accepts you as you are.

Knowing that the dark, crummy, sinful secrets of your heart are met with God's grace, what will you do in response? Perhaps today you can begin by acknowledging and confessing your sinful secrets. Transformation and a life of holiness begin with confession.

Pray

Living Lord, I confess that tucked away in my heart are secrets that don't honor you. I confess that I somehow think I can keep them from you, but the reality is, you know my heart better than I do. I confess my own brokenness and darkness, and I pray that you would begin to declutter the secrets of my heart. Examine my heart and expose my sins. I thank you that my secrets and my sins are met with your transforming grace. I thank you that my darkness is met with your illuminating, eternal love. I love you, Lord. Amen.

PALM SUNDAY

April 14, 2019

written by Jeren Rowell

Read

Luke 19:28–40

Additional: Psalm 118:1–2, 19–29

Reflect

The entrance of Jesus into Jerusalem is a high moment, yet it will come crashing into despair and defeat for these disciples in less than a week. In this moment, it seems that the messianic expectations of the people might be realized. "The whole crowd of disciples" have been shaped in an expectation that the Messiah will bring deliverance from oppression and set Israel back into a place of freedom and prosperity. Jesus seems to be acting like the king they have been waiting for, so spirits are high.

We see Jesus give his disciples specific instructions about going into the village ahead and securing a mount for the procession. It's the kind of thing conquering kings do. They come riding into the city after a great conquest to receive the accolades of the people. Jesus mounts the colt, and the parade begins. The scene is one of the most exciting and joyful in Scripture as these followers give praise to God for the hope of the coming Messiah.

No wonder these disciples think the big day has arrived. No wonder they are ready to declare the coming kingdom. One of the interesting and important features of this story is the fact that Jesus arrives as the new King not on a great white steed but on a lowly donkey. When Matthew tells the story (21:5), he links this fact to the prophecy of Zechariah: "Rejoice greatly, Daughter Zion! Shout, Daughter Jerusalem! See, your king comes to you, righteous and victorious, lowly and riding on a donkey, on a colt, the foal of a donkey" (9:9). Jesus making this entry on a donkey signals something important: this king comes not with violence and power; this king comes in peace. He comes not with force but with humility. And behind him is not an army of warriors but a small group of commoners who are called to be disciples.

He came riding on a donkey, and very few acknowledged him as Messiah. They wanted the Messiah to come. They recited the promises and prophecies. They sang the songs of hope. But they expected a king on a white horse with a sword in his hand. They did not expect their king to come riding on a donkey with healing in his hands.

Later in the week, when Jesus comes before Pilate, he will say, "My kingdom is not of this world. If it were, my servants would fight to prevent my arrest by the Jewish leaders. But now my kingdom is from another place" (John 18:36). That would be the way of earthly kings, the way of power. Can we see the implication for our time? So many Christians today seem to think that our appropriate posture toward the world is one of battle, fighting, gaining power, finding a voice—whatever we may call it, it's about trying to use power. But Jesus's followers are called to a different way. It is the way of bearing witness to the in-breaking kingdom of God; a kingdom of peace, forgiveness, and reconciliation.

A unique feature of Luke's account is the final move of the Pharisees seeking to silence the testimony of the Lord's disciples. They want Jesus to order them to stop singing their doxology. Jesus responds with a simple but profound image: "If they keep quiet, the stones will cry out." The announcement of the coming reign of God in Christ will be announced and celebrated. God will provide a witness to this world-changing event, even if that witness is nature itself.

Pray

Lord Jesus, grant us grace to see and understand your ways. We are tempted to reach to principalities and powers to secure our lives, but your ways are love, service, and peace. Help us not to be afraid to walk in your ways. In the name of the Father, Son, and Holy Spirit we pray. Amen.

Read

John 12:1–11

Additional: Psalm 36:5–11 • Isaiah 42:1–9 • Hebrews 9:11–15

Reflect

Do you consider yourself a sensible person? I like to think of myself as a person who operates in sensible and orderly ways. Even as a teen, I had a clear focus on my future. I knew God was calling me to preach. So I prepared myself for a path that would lead to college, then seminary, then into pastoral ministry. I thought my map was sensible and trustworthy. One thing my map did not include was a girlfriend, but then she came along and wouldn't you know it, my sense went right out the window!

Has something like this ever happened to you? It may simply be part of what it means to be human. What if it's also part of what it means to follow Jesus? Our passage for today is essentially about worship, and it contrasts two ways of approaching Jesus. One way is sensible, the other full of sensibility (or emotion).

This story comes at a critical point in the Gospel of John. Jesus finds himself now in a hostile environment. In chapter 11 he raised Lazarus from the dead, so one might think he would be a hero here in chapter 12. For the religious leaders, however, the raising of Lazarus was the proverbial straw that broke the camel's back. They decided that Jesus must be eliminated.

In the midst of this hostility, Martha and Mary host a dinner for Jesus. We can imagine the joy of these two sisters as their brother, who was entombed, now joins them at the dinner table. Martha is busy serving—her sensible form of worship. Mary, however, worships in a different way. John tells us at the beginning what a critical moment this is: "six days before the Passover." More than marking the calendar, he is noting the looming cross.

Without a word, Mary breaks the neck off of a perfume jar and pours the precious contents on the feet of Jesus. We can imagine the room growing still as all eyes fix on Jesus and Mary. Jesus simply watches as this woman, with tears running down her cheeks, washes his feet with this oil and wipes it off with her hair. I would not presume to understand all that moved Mary, but even I can see that there's more love here than I dare try to explain. It is a beautiful moment.

Then Judas opens his mouth. He protests that this lavish act is not sensible. The sensible thing to do would have been to sell the expensive perfume and use the proceeds—a year's worth of wages—for some good cause. And Judas isn't wrong in a factual sense. After all, Jesus cares for the poor and wants his followers to do the same. Would not each of us want to be sensible and practical too? Yet Mary, in her impractical act, may understand something about worship that we need to understand: love is not always sensible.

Judas has the sensible idea. John, of course, lets us know in plain terms that Judas actually has other motives—the kind with dollar signs in front of them—but even if Judas's heart is not pure, he is absolutely right that the perfume could've been used in a more sensible way. Yet Mary seems to understand something about practicality that Judas will never grasp (later, money will drive his actions once again, this time toward betraying Jesus and precipitating Jesus's very death). Being practical or sensible may not be the important thing right now. This is why Jesus says, "You will always have the poor among you, but you will not always have me." Jesus is not endorsing unconcern for the poor. He is simply saying to Judas, "You will never lack opportunity to serve the poor. If this is really the motive behind questioning Mary, then don't worry about it."

Perhaps the real question that Jesus presses into the heart of Judas is, *Would you dare to be impractical in your devotion to me? Would you dare to let your sensibility override your sense in your worship?*

And what Jesus asks of Judas, he may also ask of me. *I know you love to be a sensible, practical person, but would you dare to be extravagant in your worship? Would you dare to show your love for me in a way that isn't sensible?*

Mary, by her example, teaches us something about the heart of a worshiper who has surrendered self-interest. When worship is our response to the God whom we love with all our hearts, it may lead us to acts that will not always be sensible. So break open the jar, and may the fragrance of our love for Jesus fill the world.

Pray

Heavenly Father, we confess that too often we try to remain in control of our worship. Help us, by the Holy Spirit, to release fear and to become willing to be lost in wonder, love, and praise. May our worship rise from pure and grateful hearts of love. And may our lives this day bear witness to your transforming love for us. In the beautiful name of Jesus Christ, amen.

APRIL 16, 2019

written by Jeren Rowell

Read

John 12:20–36

Additional: Psalm 71:1–14 • Isaiah 49:1–7 • 1 Corinthians 1:18–31

Reflect

When I served at Chicago First Church of the Nazarene, the pulpit had the King James version of the request from John 12:21 carved into the top: "Sir, we would see Jesus." Put in our modern-day context like this—carved into the pulpit from where the Word of God is preached by both men and women—the words seem to be a directive, a reminder, to those who preach that Christian faith ought to be as simple as seeing Jesus. No need to make things complicated and heavy, Preacher; we just want to see Jesus, that's all.

Our text today opens with some people who want to see Jesus. However, notice that these people are described by John as Greeks—in other words, they are gentiles and not Jews. The final words of the preceding text are, "Look how the whole world has gone after him" (v. 19). The very next thing we hear is about some Greeks (outsiders)—"the world" coming to Jesus.

"Jesus, there are some Greeks here who want an audience with you."
What would you expect to happen next? Wouldn't you assume
Jesus would say, "Oh, there are some people who want to see
me? Fine, let's go have a talk." Can't you imagine Jesus sitting
down with them and answering their questions? After all, that
would be the simplest thing to do.

Did you notice, though, that Jesus never answers the question of
whether he will see them? This is a simple request that requires
a simple yes or no answer. Yes, Jesus will see them, or no, he
won't. But look again at verse 23: "Jesus replied, 'The hour has
come for the Son of man . . .'" What? Simple question, Jesus:
do you want to see these guys or not? Yet he launches into this
discourse on laying down his life, being glorified, and judgment
coming on the world.

This is a critical point in John's Gospel. The cross has begun to
cast a long shadow over the story. Jesus has been trying to talk
about it, but his words largely fall on deaf ears. So in this final
week, here comes "the world" (Greeks) with a simple question.
It is our question too: "Can we see Jesus? We have heard the
promise of the coming kingdom. Is it for us too? Will Messiah
save not only his people but also the whole world?"

Yes, they can see Jesus. But they will see him as the Suffering
Savior. His answer to them was, "I, when I am lifted up from
the earth, will draw all men to myself." They want to see Jesus.
Maybe they simply desire a conversation, but he responds by
pointing to his cross. This is how you ruin a good religion. You
ruin it by bringing up this cross stuff all the time. Jesus just
couldn't seem to get it off his mind.

I don't know exactly what the engravers of the Chicago First
pulpit had in mind, but I do know that, often, the Jesus we want
to see is the one who makes us feel better. We want a Jesus who
makes life simple and enjoyable. Our religion doesn't have to be
complicated, right? "We just want to see Jesus." Yet, when Jesus
talks about what God is doing in the inauguration of the kingdom of God, he points to the cross. In the image of the one who

is lifted up, we see the God who gathers into himself in the person of Jesus all of the sin, brokenness, and violence of a fallen world, takes it to death, and then delivers us out of it through resurrection and new creation.

The challenge for the church is that it's not pleasant to talk about the cross. However, unless we've encountered the cross, we have not seen Jesus. The gospel of the suffering, crucifixion, death, resurrection, and ascension of our Lord and the gift of the Spirit mean to unmask the principalities and powers to which we, even in the church, are tempted to offer our lives.

Our Holy Week temptation may be to rush past these darkening days and get on with the brightness of Easter. Yet, if we are to know a deep relationship with God, we must not avoid the reality of suffering that accompanies the countercultural Christian life. Sunday is coming, but we need the discipline of Holy Week, the appreciative awareness of Good Friday. For it's through the cross and resurrection that we are forgiven, healed, *and* made new. This is how we truly see Jesus.

Pray

Crucified Lord, grant us grace to embrace your cross. We are afraid of much that it represents, but show us that your resurrection breaks the power of canceled sin. Help us to see that only when we are buried with you in baptism can we be raised to new life. May we truly see you, high and lifted up. In praise of your glorious grace, amen.

WEDNESDAY OF HOLY WEEK

APRIL 17, 2019

written by Jeren Rowell

Read

Isaiah 50:4–9a

Additional: Psalm 70 • John 13:21–32 • Hebrews 12:1–3

Reflect

The vision Isaiah articulates in his prophetic account is about how God will redeem Israel. It is a vision of hope to a people in exile, reminding them that God has not left them but will restore them. The prophet's vision sounds wonderful. When God reigns, he says, there will be peace. God is making a road in the wilderness and streams in the desert. There will be healing and the drying of tears and many other wonderful things (see Isaiah 35, 43, 49). It is all true—but the problem is that this is all the people of God want to hear, even though it's not all that Isaiah has to say.

As Isaiah continues to talk about how God's promise of redemption will be fulfilled, the language of his vision becomes disturbing. It almost seems as if the vision itself becomes threatened when we hear the way he talks in this text. He is talking about the Servant of the Lord, the Redeemer, who will bring all of these wonderful things to pass.

What we tend to assume, and what Israel assumes, is that someone who can pull off a great restoration will have to be a strong and powerful leader; one who can overthrow governments and make military leaders bow down; one who will be revered and respected by the whole world. This is the kind of Messiah they expect.

But then, through the prophet, we hear the Servant speak, and he doesn't sound strong and overpowering. He says, "I offered my back to those who beat me, my cheeks to those who pulled out my beard; I did not hide my face from mocking and spitting." We begin to discover in Isaiah's vision that God's promise will not be fulfilled through military triumph or political power but through the brokenness of a servant. Somehow, God is going to restore God's people through what will look to the world like failure.

For we who know the gospel story, it is easy for us to say, "Well, of course; I know Jesus had to die for my sins." But suffering is not really what we expect from God most of the time. Israel doesn't expect it either, which is why they struggle to accept Jesus as the Messiah. When Jesus comes along and starts talking about suffering, crucifixion, and death, they want no part of it, but God will not do it the way they want it done. God's unbelievable answer to our need comes through the wounding of his Servant.

Jesus continually tries to point his followers to the realities of the cross, yet they cannot see. They want God to be their powerful and beautiful God. Instead they get a wounded God, hanging on a cross as a criminal. We are so easily seduced by strength, power, and beauty until we begin to conflate those things with how the Christian life should be. If God is really for us, we say, then our lives should be full of happiness, health, and blessing. And if these things do not happen, then we are tempted to grow discouraged and disappointed with God.

Jesus says, "Unless a kernel of wheat falls to the ground and dies, it remains only a single seed. But if it dies, it produces many seeds" (John 12:24). Jesus also says, "Whoever wants to save their life will lose it, but whoever loses their life for me will find it" (Matt. 16:25). There it is. Brokenness, letting go, coming to the end of yourself—the cross. This is what the season of Lent calls us toward.

Perhaps an important Lenten question is, *What is my response when difficulty comes into my life?* Our temptation in those moments is to become faithless and angry. We can be honest with God about the emotions we are feeling, but the gospel shows us that suffering does not mean God has turned away. In fact, it could be that sharing in the sufferings of Christ (Rom. 8:17) may teach us some of the deepest lessons there are to be learned in the way of Jesus. This is not to say that God causes bad things to happen to us in order to teach us. This is simply the gospel truth that God is working to redeem all things. Therefore, suffering can be redeemed into formation in Christlikeness.

Maybe the question is: Can we trust God to transform our pain, our brokenness, into the very life of Christ?

Pray

Lord, we bring to you our disappointment and anger over the things in life that have not turned out as we hoped. Save us from bitterness and doubt. Help us to see how you are at work to redeem even the painful experiences of our lives. Thank you for the model of the One who laid down his life for us. Keep us in the peace of Christ. Amen.

MAUNDY THURSDAY

April 18, 2019

written by Jeren Rowell

Read

John 13:1–17, 31b–35

Additional: Exodus 12:1–14 • Psalm 116:1–2, 12–19 •
1 Corinthians 11:23–26

Reflect

Some years ago, the National Institute of Mental Health conducted a fascinating experiment. It took place in a nine-foot-square cage designed to house about 160 mice. For two and a half years, the colony of mice grew from 8 to 2,200. There was an abundance of food, water, and other resources. All mortality factors (except aging) were virtually eliminated. But as the mice population reached its peak in that controlled colony, the research psychologist began to notice some unusual behaviors.

Adults formed groups of about a dozen. In these groups, different mice performed particular social functions. The males, who normally would protect their own territory, withdrew from leadership and became uncharacteristically passive. The females became unusually aggressive and forced out the young. The young found themselves without a place in the community, and they grew to be increasingly self-indulgent. They ate, drank, slept, and groomed themselves but showed no normal assertiveness. In short, the whole mouse society became disrupted, and after five years, all the mice had died even though there was an abundance of food, water, resources, and an absence of disease.

What researchers noted from that experiment was that the gradual move toward self-reliance and isolation—an "every mouse for himself" bias—is what killed the society. Sound familiar?

Our world has become a large, impersonal, and busy place. Although we are more connected than ever in terms of technology, we are also more isolated and lonely than ever. We are pushed together but uninvolved. Neighbors no longer visit over the back fence. The automatic garage door keeps us from having to encounter the people who live around us. We occupy common space but have little authentic relationship. We are finding out what happens to a society when people orient their lives toward self-interest.

Jesus makes it clear that our calling is to follow his example and to orient our lives not to being served but to serving others. This wonderful picture of Jesus in John 13 teaches us not only the activity of a servant but, more importantly, the attitude of a servant.

The disciples thought of everything in putting together this dinner, except for one thing. They forgot to provide for the customary washing of feet. The dinner hour has come, and now what are they going to do? None of them can stoop to such a menial task, after all—they have just been arguing about which of them will be the greatest in this new kingdom! So Jesus takes the towel and the basin and begins to demonstrate naturally and without fanfare the work of a true minister.

This is more than a timely illustration. This act comes out of Jesus's heart. It is one thing to act like a servant, quite another to be a servant. We need to note the place from which this posture of service arises: "Jesus knew . . . that he had come from God and was returning to God; so he got up . . ." Jesus can embrace his calling because he knows who he is.

We can only embrace our calling if we know who we are in Christ; if we know that our value and our authority do not come from position or acclamation but from the smile of a Father who sees what is done in secret. This is the heart of Jesus.

John Wesley's Covenant Service is finding renewed place among us in recent years. It is a beautiful liturgy of renewing our covenant in Christ. Toward the conclusion of the service, the covenant prayer that is shared by the gathered community says, in part:

Make us what you will, Lord, and send us where we are to go.
Let us be vessels of silver or gold, or vessels of wood or stone;
as long as we are vessels of honor we are content.
If we are not the head, or the eye, or the ear,
one of the nobler and more honorable instruments,
then let us be the hands, or the feet,
as one of the lowest and least esteemed of all the servants of our
    Lord.

As we follow the path of Jesus in this Holy Week, we must examine our hearts and ask: Are we honestly willing to say to the Lord Jesus, "Whatever you want to do with me, however you want to use me, here I am"? Our calling is to be a servant like Jesus.

Pray

Spirit of God, this world teaches us to protect ourselves and to care mostly for ourselves. Teach us the way of Jesus, who "did not regard equality with God as something to be exploited, but emptied himself, taking the form of a slave" (Phil. 2:6b–7a, NRSV). Free us from the fear that in serving others we will be diminished. May we learn the joy of a life lived in service to others. In the name of Jesus Christ, the Servant of all. Amen.

GOOD FRIDAY

April 19, 2019

written by Jeren Rowell

Read

John 18:1–19:42

Additional: Psalm 22 • Isaiah 52:13–53:12 • Hebrews 4:14–16;
5:7–9 or Hebrews 10:16–25

Reflect

This Gospel text has much to do with the question of what it means to be king. What does it mean to be subject to a king? What does it mean to be part of a kingdom? These questions bring us to the palace of Pilate, one who certainly imagines himself to be a person of authority—a king, of sorts. This scene occurs because the folks who arrested Jesus in the garden are looking for someone with enough authority and courage to carry out their dark intentions. Enter Pilate, who really tries to appear in charge. He summons Jesus into his presence. That's what kings do: they summon people.

Although Pilate is trying to be in charge, his attempt to interrogate Jesus is about to turn right back onto him. The question is, "Who is Lord?" Pilate—representing his superior, Caesar (the actual king of Rome)—imagines this question has been settled.

If Jesus is claiming to be a king, this is a problem for Caesar, and what is a problem for Caesar is a problem for Pilate. But Jesus is working at something much deeper than politics. Jesus is working at the heart, which is why this conversation becomes so troubling for Pilate. Jesus keeps poking Pilate with questions of faith and truth, but Pilate can't imagine truth outside of the systems of power.

"My kingdom is not of this world," Jesus says. In fact, he says it twice in verse 36. And then Jesus says something very interesting that may have profound implication for us. He says, "If my kingdom were from this world, my followers would be fighting to keep me from being handed over" (NRSV).

Can you see what this means for us? Jesus's followers are called to the way of truth. Jesus says, "The reason I was born and came into the world is to testify to the truth." Jesus imagines lordship differently than does the world: it's about truth rather than power. The real question now is what Pilate asks in verse 38: "What is truth?"

Many in our world assume Pilate's question to be unanswerable. Truth will not be discovered through Pilate's interrogation. Truth will not be discovered through any kind of reasoning or even through religion. Truth is standing before him. This is the one of whom John said in the opening of this Gospel, "In the beginning was the Word, and the Word was with God, and the Word was God."

So Jesus, who is Truth, says to Pilate, "Everyone who belongs to the truth listens to my voice" (NRSV). Pilate is worried about threats to power and political authority, but that's not what Jesus is concerned with. Kingdoms, when they function well, are places of order, security, and provision. These are things we all desire and need, but whom do we trust to provide these things? For us to say "Jesus is Lord" is to affirm that, even though we enjoy some very good things that come from earthly kingdoms, our real security and hope are not in any nation on earth. For us to say "Jesus is Lord" is to allow every decision and priority of our lives to come under the scrutiny of whether we are living to serve ourselves or to serve God by loving our neighbor as ourselves. For us to say "Jesus is Lord" is to proclaim to the principalities and powers of our time, "My hope is built on nothing less than Jesus's blood and righteousness."

This text on Good Friday calls us to remember not only that Jesus gave himself on the cross for our salvation as individuals, for which we give thanks to God; but Jesus also died to break the bonds of the principalities and powers that enslave all nations, and to establish a kingdom that is not *of* this world but is breaking *into* this world as the universal rule and reign of God in Christ Jesus by the power of the Holy Spirit. Good Friday is not only about the forgiveness of *my* sins. Good Friday is also about the freedom that includes deliverance from every worldly idea and construct of what makes for a good king and places us in "the kingdom of our Lord and of his Messiah" (Rev. 11:15).

Pray

Our Father, we cannot express adequately our gratitude for the gift of your Son, our Lord Jesus Christ. We praise you for the forgiveness of sins and for life everlasting. We also thank you for delivering us as your people from the dominion of darkness and enabling us, in Christ, to announce the good news of your reign over all the earth and your work to redeem all things. Through Jesus Christ our crucified, risen, and ascended Lord, amen.

HOLY SATURDAY

April 20, 2019

written by Jeren Rowell

Read

Matthew 27:57–66

Additional: Job 14:1–14 or Lamentations 3:1–9, 19–24 •
Psalm 31:1–4, 15–16 • John 19:38–42 • 1 Peter 4:1–8

Reflect

The burial of Jesus is part of our confession of faith in the
Apostles' Creed: "he was crucified, died, and was buried." It is
important not because we glorify the death in itself but because
we believe and confess that the death was real; therefore, the
resurrection is real. It was necessary for the church to certify
the death of Jesus because of the efforts to discredit the claims
of resurrection. In this story, the religious leaders remind Pilate
that Jesus claimed he would rise again, which, in their view,
would only make the "Jesus problem" worse than before. Evi-
dently Pilate agrees, so he does their work for them by ordering
the securing of the tomb.

In contrast to this anxiety, the wordless testimony of Joseph is
a powerful feature of this story. Joseph has become a disciple of
the Lord Jesus yet still functions within the privileged class of

the rich and is, according to Mark, "a respected member of the council" (15:43, NRSV). Perhaps at some personal risk, Joseph simply does what needs to be done when all other options are exhausted. It's the kind of thing we do when a loved one dies. We prepare the body, we gather, we look, we struggle to find any words, so we cry and hug one another, and we prepare food. We don't know what else to do, so we give ourselves to the liturgies of death. And it's important that we do these things.

In his commentary on the book of Matthew, Dr. Roger Hahn notes that this story of Joseph and the women who watched the burial says something about the place of all gifts and roles in the kingdom of God. We tend to think most of disciples like Peter, James, and John, who are the leaders. Yet these leaders often fail, and Matthew shows us in the quiet actions of Joseph and the women that all of us can "contribute what we have to the cause of the kingdom."

It would be a mistake for us to give in to our temptation during Holy Week to rush past the silence of Saturday. On Holy Saturday (or Easter Vigil), the church should do the things that people do when loved ones die and we are left with the uncomfortable awareness of our mortality, our inability to save ourselves, and our struggle to comfort those who mourn—especially ourselves. So we come together, and we wait.

There is something necessary about the wordless waiting of Holy Saturday. There is something important about being reminded that we are helpless in the face of death, incapable of securing our own lives. We are utterly dependent on the grace and power of God to break the chains of death and to bring life where we would only be able to expect death.

So on Saturday, we gather without saying very much. We face our mortality, and we face our sin. We sit in awe of a God who, in Christ, "humbled himself and became obedient to the point of death—even death on a cross" (Phil. 2:8, NRSV).

Pray

Holy Father, we wait upon your mercy, grace, and power to redeem us from the grave through the resurrection of your Son, our Lord Jesus Christ. Grant us courage to face the outcomes of the cross and the reality of our Lord's death. And grant us hope that teaches us to believe that you are able to raise new life, even when all we can see is death. We trust in you, holy and sovereign triune God. Amen.

EASTER SUNDAY

April 21, 2019

written by Jeren Rowell

Read

John 20:1–18

Additional: Psalm 118:1–2, 14–24 • Isaiah 65:17–25 •
Luke 24:1–12 • Acts 10:34–43 • 1 Corinthians 15:19–26

Reflect

It is Easter, so we expect that our Bible reading for today would
be about the resurrection of our Lord Jesus. However, there is
always a challenge for us when we read familiar texts. Our tendency is to stop hearing them. We fairly preoccupy the hearing
with our previous experience. However, what if there is a fresh
experience for us in the truth of this text? For each of us, no
matter how we have come to another Easter Sunday, there is an
important question to answer: What do you see?

Did you notice how seeing runs through this account? The scene
opens with Mary going to the tomb and *seeing* that the stone
door has been removed. She runs to tell Peter and "the other
disciple," who *sees* the limp linens lying there. Then Peter bursts
into the tomb and *sees* the linens and head covering folded and

neatly placed. Then the first disciple comes into the tomb and *sees* and believes.

In Matthew's telling of the story, there are additional notes about seeing. The angel says to them that he knows they are looking for Jesus. Then the greatest announcement of all time: "He is not here; he has risen, just as he said" (28:6). Then the angel invites them to "come and *see*" the place where he lay. *Investigate it for yourself. See with your own eyes that he has risen from the dead.* Then the angel instructs them to go to Galilee because there they will *see* the risen Christ.

As the Gospel writers frame this central story in terms of seeing, perhaps the question with which we need to wrestle anew each Easter is: What does it mean to see? This is a thematic question throughout the Gospels. Having eyes to see the reality of the resurrection is more than being presented with a set of facts. The physical evidence of an empty tomb will not convince anyone. The empty tomb is not presented as proof but as a sign. This is a faith story.

When we profess our faith we say, "I believe in the resurrection of the body and life everlasting." This affirmation makes all the difference on the Monday after Resurrection Sunday, and all the days after that. It enables us to see in a whole new way. For, if God in Christ is redeeming the whole creation, then we go forward not in fear but in hope.

If Christ is indeed "the firstfruits" of resurrection of all "who have fallen asleep" (1 Cor. 15:20), then we do not grieve like those who "have no hope" (1 Thess. 4:13). If Christ is risen, then we are "more than conquerors through him who loved us" (Rom. 8:37). This is all much more than someday wishful thinking; this is the foundation on which we now stand and the future into which we boldly stride. In Matthew's narrative, the angel tells the women about the place where they will see resurrection. The angel says, "He is not here . . . he is going ahead of you to Galilee; there you will see him" (28:6, 7, NRSV).

Perhaps the mention of Galilee is much more than geography but also theology. No matter what life holds; no matter what we must face at home, school, or work; no matter what uncertainties the future may hold, the good news of Easter is that the risen Christ has already gone ahead of us. He is there, occupying that space, redeeming it with his presence and power. And this is where the question of seeing or not seeing really matters.

So on Easter, I would ask you: Are you willing to see the reality of the risen Christ tomorrow? Are you willing to see him in every decision, every action, and every thought of your life? Are you willing to acknowledge that Jesus wants to be more to you than a convenient deity you worship on Sunday or pray to when you're in trouble? The risen Lord Jesus wants to be your constant and abiding Friend, Teacher, Savior, and Lord.

The apostle Paul writes, "If you confess with your mouth that Jesus is Lord and believe in your heart that God raised him from the dead, you will be saved" (Romans 10:9, ESV).

On this Easter Sunday, I invite you to offer this prayer to God with genuine faith: *Father, I know that my sins have separated me from you. I am truly sorry, and now I want to turn away from sin and live my life totally in your direction. Please forgive me and keep me from sin. I believe that your Son, Jesus Christ, died for me, lives again, and hears my prayer. So, I invite you, Jesus, to become the forgiver and leader of my life from this day forward. Amen.*

Benediction

Now may the God of peace, who through the blood of the eternal covenant brought back from the dead our Lord Jesus, that great Shepherd of the sheep, equip you with everything good for doing his will, and may he work in us what is pleasing to him, through Jesus Christ, to whom be glory for ever and ever. Amen.
(Hebrews 13:20–21)